# LIVING THE BEAUTY DREAM

## JANET STACEY

**with**

## LIONEL PYRAH

**First British Serial Rights**

**(Excluding Electronic Rights)**

*Janet Stacey*

*[signature]*

# LIVING THE BEAUTY DREAM

Second Edition

ISBN 978-1-909424-16-6

Edited by Lionel Henry Pyrah

Launched

Bentley Baptist Church, Shakespeare Road, Doncaster

November 2012

Typeset, printed and bound in Great Britain by;

*www.direct-pod.com*

'Living the Beauty Dream'

**This book is dedicated to the memory of
Janet's mother RUTH MILNER who
died 21st May 1999.**

*Picture of Parents Wilfred and Ruth Milner
by Hugh Greaves*

'Living the Beauty Dream'

## EXPLANATORY NOTE

Whereas every effort has been made to achieve accuracy in presenting the facts correctly in this work, the author apologises for any discrepancies which may later come to light.

'Living the Beauty Dream'

# PREFACE

Today, I live in a detached three bed-roomed bungalow overlooking a small picturesque garden in Doncaster. To the rear is a bridle path, which leads to scenic Cusworth Hall, which has enraptured my heart since I first moved to the town.

Cusworth Hall has always been a favourite 'thinking' place of mine ever since I came to Doncaster thirty years ago. The hall makes me think of times gone by when my family used to be employed at stately homes as cook's, maid's and tweenies. Now I can walk in its grounds and rooms as I wish.

Old trees have been replaced with new ones, and the lake has been restored to its former glory by the local council.

All this is a far cry from Halifax, the town in which I grew up. But it was Halifax, along with Cusworth, which have helped to provide the inspiration for this book.

Every morning, I used to walk to my place of employment at Halifax sewage works, through Savile Park, the adjacent moor, and past the hospital before descending Salterhebble Hill.

I would marvel at the beauty of the crocuses, daffodils and tulips growing in the grass verges all around The Moor and the General Hospital. And during more leisurely moments, I would amble along the undulating scenery at nearby Norland moor.

Coupled with the events of my career on the catwalk, I decided from the start "no nude or topless" hence the title with "no bling" added, as in the 70's, it was all the rage for beautiful women to divulge their real female form, not me. It was a fight with journalists and agencies alike often losing contracts in the process of maintaining decency. Myself, as a child, teenager, photographic

'Living the Beauty Dream'

and catwalk model and, finally, beautician are combined into one story.

My mother suggested I write this as therapy to remind myself of what I had achieved in my youth; these memories had disappeared due to electric convulsive therapy treatment in hospital after my second baby. This book has been written from chronological notes on cuttings in my scrapbook, which my mother kept during my days as a beauty queen.

For a moment, I glance at the cover picture on the top of my mother's wall unit and think back to the day when Dennis Lever took the cover photograph at the Halifax Assembly Rooms.

Another glance takes me to Mum's picture on an adjoining shelf; I pick it up and begin to cry tears of joy. It has been over 13 years since she passed away, in May 1999, and I still ,miss her very much. As I look deeper into the picture I see Dad snapping it outside the boarding house at Lytham-St-Anne's, saying,

"Come on Ruth, give us a smile".

She was so shy and reserved and would only let Dad take her picture. He took one in July 1986 before he sadly departed this life six months later on 13th January 1987.

They were very content together and so much in love, just like Darby and Joan.

But Mum and I were opposites: she was shy but I was rather outgoing. My one ambition in life was to be famous and I loved every minute in front of a camera.

The Lord blessed me with a pretty face when I was young and an able mind as I grew older.

For these, I shall always be grateful to Him.

Janet Stacey
November, 2012

# ACKNOWLEDGEMENTS

I would like to place on record my grateful thanks to my dear departed parents for their guidance and comments on my acting and modelling performances, especially in my early years. Between them, they gave me great confidence and I would never have considered stepping onto a stage without their loving support. Indeed, my parents and ex-husband wholeheartedly encouraged me at the many events I took part in.

Moreover, the late Arthur Stead, my headmaster at Stead's Commercial College, set my feet on the right path for life and Tony Roach, my mathematics tutor at Doncaster College, has to be congratulated on displaying endless patience with me! And heartfelt thanks also to Alan Mattinson, my computer tutor, for the countless references he has written on my behalf. I would not have succeeded without their help.

Among many others who have assisted me during my 'beauty' years were Dennis Lever, an accomplished amateur photographer who began taking pictorial records of me from the age of 18; David Glendenning, another photographer, who took the first published picture of me which appeared in Photo News, and my mentor, Diane Parker, a valued friend on the beauty circuit.

In addition, I wish to thank Lionel Pyrah for his significant assistance in compiling and editing my story.

And lastly, I am indebted to my fiancé John Smith for his comments, consideration and counselling, all of which have helped to bring this publication to fruition.

Janet Stacey
November, 2012

## PHOTOGRAPHIC ACKNOWLEDGEMENTS

# CHAPTERS

'Living the Beauty Dream'

# CHAPTER 1
# THE HALIFAX FACTOR

A chance remark about smoking during a conversation with my boyfriend John as we were enjoying dinner one evening at my home in Doncaster led me to reflect on those halcyon days of the Sixties and Seventies when I used to parade along with many other like-minded girls on the catwalks of ballrooms and swimming pools the length and breadth of the kingdom.

After landing a position as a promotions girl with Players Number Six - who, curiously, only wanted to recruit non-smokers to their ranks – I reluctantly left the undulating slopes of West Yorkshire for the flatlands of South Yorkshire in 1970, the year of my marriage.

My journey south-eastwards seems a long way away now from my formative years living in the foothills of the Pennines in Halifax.

A great deal has happened to me in those four decades and my hometown certainly played its part in shaping my career.

Indeed, this famous mill town, and, in particular, the statue of Diana in People's Park, was to inspire me sufficiently to pursue a career in the beauty business in my teens and twenties.

Halifax is pleasant and engaging, and largely stone-built with a tree-lined square at its centre from which all its main streets radiated, Halifax possessed thoroughfares which accommodated a particular trade, whereas George Square contained the entire town's leisure sales facilities, together with the bus station.

Such was my interest in the town that I would often saunter around the impressive Victorian buildings which housed the many banks, offices and shops that provided its commercial heartbeat whilst close by Commercial Street were the clothing shops and the market area through which I would browse endlessly.

The town's prosperity was based on the woollen industry and Halifax certainly had its share of carpet mills in the 19th century but nowadays the shells of these once-mighty structures are home to craft firms.

Opulence, too, was reflected in the town's jewel in the crown - the splendidly ornate Piece Hall, which still draws visitors from all over the world to sample its unique atmosphere.

One particular structure missing in my day, but now happily restored, was the gibbet. I mention this in passing as I was often told the tale of this locally famous object. Dad would inform me with relish that, in the Middle Ages, people were beheaded for stealing sheep and that this fact gave rise to the equally famous saying, 'From Hull, Hell and Halifax, Good Lord, deliver us'. It is with a certain fondness, therefore, that I am pleased to recall my days in Halifax where I spent many happy hours crossing the expansive grassed area known locally as The Moor, which skirts Saville Park, an area rich in Victorian residences.

But it was People's Park which served to provide the inspiration for my career ambitions, containing as it still does a magnificent collection of statues of Greek gods and goddesses along its splendid promenade.

It was whilst walking with Dad through the park that he once turned to me and said that I reminded him of the goddess Diana. This was an apt remark as she was a huntress - and I was born under the zodiacal sign of Sagittarius the Archer!

The ornate statues which overlook the park's beautiful rose gardens continue to produce sweet-smelling aromas all summer long. Dad and I enjoyed the works of Nature and when I was growing up there seemed no better place to appreciate them than this picturesque spot.

*Picture of Janet Milner at 18 months by Hugh Greaves*

# CHAPTER 2
# MY EARLY YEARS

I was born on the eighth of December 1946 at Heathroyd, a small nursing home on Francis Street in the King Cross district of Halifax, the only daughter of Wilfred and Ruth Milner. Today, this building serves as the gatehouse of Princess Mary High School.

Mum often recounted to me the tale of how, after my birth, Dad, being very pleased to have a daughter, accidentally tripped over a low wall outside the nursing home; he had not been imbibing, by the way! On picking himself up, he sat down on the wall and lit his pipe to collect his thoughts. Then after contemplating a while on Mum's suggestion regarding my name – her choice was Janet Elizabeth – decided simply on Janet, after Miss Janet Fairburn, the nurse who had assisted Dr Victor Mayer at my birth. Dad then headed straight to the Registrar of 'Hatches, Matches and Despatches' to make it so!

My spiritual well-being was catered for soon after with baptism at Warley Clough Methodist Chapel in June 1947. Dad's cousin, Pauline Milner, had been chosen as my godmother prior to the ceremony, which was conducted by the then priest-in-charge, the Reverend Evans.

My first home was number seven Byron Avenue, a two bed-roomed terraced property in nearby Sowerby Bridge, but being only twelve months old and a mere babe in arms I could never recall it.

My parents later returned to Halifax and to my childhood home of 249 King Cross, where Dad established his radio, television and electrical repairs business.

Here, the accommodation was very different as the property came complete with a brewery tenancy from the Prince of Wales public house next door!

Mum's first words to Dad when he proposed starting the business were: "Don't you think that I'm moving there; it's not a nice place to bring up a little girl". She had a point as there was an outside toilet in the pub yard!

Dad had his way, though, and we moved to the two-up and two-down premises. My parents converted the front room of the house into a shop which boasted an office behind a partition, the kitchen becoming the dining/repair room.

Upstairs were two palatial bedrooms and an attic, the front bedroom being converted into a lounge whilst the back bedroom divided into two bedrooms. At first, my cot was placed in the alcove but as I grew, I was 'promoted' to a single bed, a dividing plasterboard wall being erected for Mum and Dad's privacy!

When I was 12, however, Mum decided on some alterations, following which a kitchenette was added to the two rooms on the first floor. Then I got a double bed because the front room was larger than the back room.

But after the work was completed, the front room, which had been the lounge, suddenly became the bedroom – and the back room, formerly the bedroom, became the lounge.

You may be wondering, though, as to what happened to the plasterboard wall. I have to inform you that it was demolished only to be rebuilt and positioned in the front room to accommodate the kitchen, which now overlooked the lounge from an alcove over the steps which connected it to the bedroom through a private door.

Reflecting on my childhood, I must confess to having chosen Mum and Dad well! They showed love and affection for me when I was young and were always there to support me in later years, especially when I took to the beauty circuit.

I was always very fond of my family and was particularly interested in their history. For this reason, I trust you will indulge me as I relate a little about them to you.

My paternal grandma's name was Ackroyd, whose descendants originated from Bradford, where they were engaged in the weaving trade.

Granddad Milner, a railwayman, was a joiner in his spare time during weekdays but exchanged his brace and bit for linament and a magic sponge on Saturdays as he tended injured players of Halifax Town Football Club at The Shay.

My maternal granddad, Ion Keague, could be said to have experienced a more romantic - albeit precarious - lifestyle as a sergeant in, so I was told, the Third Dragoon Guards. Granddad served in Ireland and South Africa and took part in the Boer War winning a bravery award and other medals.

Elsewhere, my grandma Gertrude Keague followed a more genteel career managing a Halifax bakery. Her relations were Protestants from the Dutch province of Brabant who later settled in France before moving to Kent in 1764. Today, however, my cousins are involved in market gardening but still reside in the Canterbury area.

My Mum had three brothers; Jack, Robert (known as Bob), William (nicknamed Bill), and three sisters, the eldest being Gertrude (Cis), Evangeline (Eva) and the youngest, Ada Elizabeth (Betty). Grandma doted on Betty, not only because she was the baby of the family but also because Granddad died three months after Betty was born.

Mum always felt, though, that she was perhaps the victim of some 'favouritism' as her sister Betty was allowed piano and singing lessons whilst she was not! In the event, Mum turned to Eva as a sisterly friend, who nearly always sided with her in any 'arguments' at home. And although, on her own admission, she would never have hit the heights as a singer, Mum possessed an enviable skill as a ballroom dancer in her adult years.

Confectionery was Mum's chosen career path whilst Dad, who had been an RAF navigator and RADAR assistant whilst serving King and Country, trained after the war as an electrical engineer - a move which was to be of benefit to him later on once he embraced the commercial world by opening his own business, acquiring rented premises from Ramsdens' brewery.

And to complete the Milner enterprise, his brother Vincent, who had trained as an accountant, worked with Dad whilst Mum helped with merchandising. On Sundays, I usually went to morning service with my parents before attending Sunday school straight afterwards. The three of us would then go for our weekly walk, occasionally calling on Grandma Milner, who lived at Ovenden in the town.

We would walk from King Cross, through People's Park and Boothtown, before finally arriving at her house in time for tea. But sometimes, Dad would take me to a local beauty spot at Norland where we both enjoyed the view from Ladstone Rock.

Meanwhile, on the education front, my first school was Parkinson Lane Primary, an establishment I enjoyed. However, it holds one bad memory for me; I became the victim of a cruel needlework teacher, who would stick needles into my fingers as a punishment for making mistakes during embroidery classes.

But when I was five-and-a-half, my parents transferred me to Miss Oakley's Primary, an all-girls' establishment with female teachers. Amongst the friends I made there were Mirabelle Moore, Susan Nicholl and Georgina Lord and I recall we were all given French names; Georgina was Odette whilst I became Colette. Years later, I named my eldest daughter Helen Odette in memory of this friendship.

Miss Oakley's school was a pleasant place where we revelled in each other's company in a relaxed atmosphere, the highlight being Miss Bearpark's dancing lessons every Tuesday and Thursday. One of the pupils at the dancing school was Angela Hughes, who I am pleased to count among my friends and who I still see to this day.

Miss Bearpark must have thought that Angela and I had reached an acceptable dancing standard under her tutelage as we were invited to accompany her to Rishworth Grammar School to act as partners for some of the budding Fred Astaires there.  But oh, how we enjoyed these experiences, dashing across the room to many a Scottish or Irish reel.

 During this period Mum and I made regular visits to Halifax Royal Infirmary for a new antibiotic treatment in an effort to clear up my nagging bronchitis, which was causing me to have breathing problems. These attacks would recur every seven years throughout my life – and I 'looked forward' to them with much trepidation as you can imagine!.

Whilst on the subject of shortage of breath, I was informed years later that people who live in stone-built houses are more prone to contracting bronchitis. Now, I cannot properly vouch for the authenticity of this statement except to relate that I lived in three stone houses throughout my childhood!

As a child, of course, I enjoyed being entertained and when I was seven, I would visit one of the local cinemas with Dad, usually on Mondays, whilst

Mum entertained her female friends.

There were five cinemas in Halifax in those days: the Palladium, Gaumont, Odeon, Regal and Pioneer (later the Electric), but, sadly, only the Regal, renamed the ABC, shows films now whilst the Odeon is a bingo hall. Indeed, it was the Odeon where I remember, as a teenager, seeing those great performers of the Sixties and Seventies, Bert Weedon, The Beatles, Cliff Richard, Acker Bilk and his Jazzmen, and the Temperance Seven.

But earlier, when I was 10, I had a wonderful summer holiday – a 10-day treat with my aunt Eva in London on a Wallace Arnold tour. It is something of a distant memory now but I well remember visiting the Tower of London where I gazed in wonder at the Crown Jewels.

We also went to St Paul's Cathedral and the church of St Martin's-in-the-Fields - and even took in the Pudding Lane monument, before finishing with a trip to the Royal Mews and Windsor Castle.

I have to confess, though, that the highlight for me was celebrating being the youngest member of the tour. And by way of a 'present' for being just that, a visit to the Royal Mews was my 'reward' – and a seat in the Lord Mayor's coach too, from which I waved like the Queen at my companions.

Little did I think that ten years later I would be parading around Halifax as the town's Carnival Queen atop a garlanded float – and waving to the crowds!

I finally left Miss Oakley's at the age of eight, after many happy years and became a pupil at Lightcliffe High School, along with my cousin Christine

Milner, and Francis Hudson, my best friend there.

Francis had learning difficulties, I enjoyed helping her with her studies: the experience was to stand me in good stead when, 50 years on, I now help students with special needs in a professional capacity as a learning support assistant.

I have always thought life can be curious and I still maintain that belief, especially when I occasionally see three other friends from my early days in Halifax. One is Jean Armstrong who now lives in Doncaster where she is currently Secretary of the Little Theatre Company in the town.

At Lightcliffe, Francis introduced me to her sister Jane and her friend Margaret Boothroyd, who were both in the sixth form when I joined the school. I got on well with my new friends and their companionship helped me to settle quickly. At the school, my class prefect in later years was Andrew Gordon Stacey, known then as 'Teacher's Pet' – who later became my husband.

I well remember my favourite tutor was Mr Uttley, who taught mathematics and athletics – until my first crush occurred. A certain Mr Fitton, an aptly-named, tall, blonde French master, who, at over six feet tall, had to duck under the classroom doors to make his entrances, and his exits, injury-free! Mr Uttley, a regular customer at Dad's shop, used to take me to local parkland in the village, named The Stray, where he put me through my paces – for the races: the 220 yards, the 440 yards and the mile, to be exact.

He would stand with his stop watch shouting words of encouragement such as, "Come on Janet, you can do it," and "Faster, faster" as I tried to knock off vital seconds. His dedication to my cause proved somewhat fruitful in the end as I secured third spot in the mile in the 1958 school sports competition.

The headmaster at Lightcliffe was Mr Archibald Watkins, who taught geometry and algebra, whilst he wife tutored the girls in domestic science. Mr Utterly was in charge of mathematics, Mr. Fitton being responsible for English, French, Latin, German and history.

But there was plenty of variety too, with drama, music, sewing and elocution also on the curriculum. Being something of a sporty type, in addition to my favourite pursuit of athletics, I enjoyed partaking in hockey games, cricket and rounders matches.

And as far as innocent 'extra-mural' activities were concerned, it was not just the masters who could 'cut a dash' with the girls; the boys too, were not averse to showing they had an eye for the opposite sex. In fact, on many occasions we would regularly encounter groups of teenage males popping out of the bushes trying to steal a kiss or two as we passed by on our way to the sports field!

But, of course, life was not all sweetness and light during my schooldays as I recall once on the home front. One night, thieves broke into Dad's shop and I heard the thud very clearly. I had the room above the premises and soon realised we were being burgled. I rose quickly and made my way to the top of the stairs where I could hear some movement below.

After waking Dad we went downstairs together only to find that the burglars had gone.

Dad searched for the point of entry and discovered the felons had used a brick to break the shop window before making off with nine transistor radios and my Dr. Barnardo's box from the counter.

Dad rang the police and on their arrival we were both interviewed for our accounts of events. But our efforts were to no avail in the end – and we later discovered two similar incidents had occurred that night but, unfortunately, no one was ever caught.

At Lightcliffe, punishment of students, if they misbehaved, was administered by the subject tutor – usually 'six of the best' with either a cane or a slipper. Caning was the preserve of the headmaster and took place either in his office or, if someone was a regular offender, in school assembly.

When I was 12, I began entering singing contests with my cousin Jennifer Cliffe. I was a mezzo-soprano whilst Jennifer had a fine soprano voice and, together, we attended musical festivals held in the neighbouring towns of Huddersfield, Ilkley and Otley. For the record, as I recall, Jennifer usually came first, which was not surprising. Occasionally, I was placed second. Now, that was surprising!

It was around this time that I started visiting the Palladium cinema on Saturday afternoons with some of my friends who lived locally. One boy in our group was Paul Meskeyman, whose grandfather was the tenant of the Oddfellow's Arms, which my house overlooked.

During the summer holidays, Paul and I helped my father deliver television sets. I shall never forget that young Mr Meskeyman gave me my first 'serious' kiss at the age of 13 in the back of my father's van – and very nice it was too. The kiss wasn't bad either!

At that time I collected photographs of royalty and always considered Prince Charles to be good-looking, and even tried to find boys who were similar to him physically, always dreaming some day my prince would come.

But rambles too have always held my interest and on autumn weekends, Mum, Dad and I would pick blackberries with our family friends, the Johnsons, or walk with the Moores and O'Rorokes, who were members of both the Youth Hostelling Association and the Young Christians Association.

It was around this period that Mum and Dad became worried as to which career I might choose. Eventually, after due consideration, it was decided that I should attend Stead's Commercial College in Brighouse to train as a secretary.

At the college I made several friends and spent many hours of joyful study under Mr and Mrs Stead, who were like second parents to me, as far as advice and guidance were concerned. And because of this, I was able to obtain employment when I finished there.

Scholastically, I preferred English, history and languages – and I was certainly more proficient in those than I was in mathematics. To be honest, I would have been better employed drinking battery acid for all the good that particular subject did for me!

I enjoyed my spell at the college where I spent three of my teenage years – from 13 to 16 – and it was there that I learned shorthand and typing, English language and literature, and drama, this particular discipline proving invaluable in later years for me.

In those days a particularly memorable period each year was the preparation for the Nativity plays, especially when everyone had to 'adapt' their own costumes. We had great fun with the many items of clothing we had to sort out but I always thought the applause received at the end of each of the thrice-nightly shows was the icing on the cake; it gave a great lift to the confidence of everyone taking part in the productions – and provided useful training for my catwalk career.

But Mum and Dad decided I needed an occupation and thought a career in the world of local government would be a suitable option. I would have rather been a preacher, though, as I was interested in religion and the church.

But life is not all about toiling away as leisure has a role, too. And is it not said that all work and no play make Jill a dull girl?

Like all families we enjoyed our breaks and for the Milners' these were usually spent on the east coast during the last two weeks in July when the local wakes weeks were taken.

Hundreds of workers from the 'heavy woollen' district would descend on the popular resorts of Scarborough, Filey, Bridlington, and Whitby when the local woollen mills closed for the summer break.

Consequently, Halifax became very quiet and so Dad would 'shut up shop' and the three of us would decamp on the 'Yorkshire Riviera' for our annual seaside trip.

Thankfully, at least as far as Mum and Dad were concerned, fantasy gave way to reality as their only daughter eventually landed a job. And what a job it was!

On leaving school at 16, I was lucky enough (!) to be employed as a junior clerk in the sewage purification department of the local council where my duties involved opening and distributing mail, and checking vehicles at the weighbridge.

Specifically, the lorries I weighed carried sludge, mixed with chemicals in a sterilization process which, in turn, resulted in an amalgam, loosely termed manure, and the product, you will be delighted to learn, was named 'Organifax'. Other vans I weighed would carry oil extracted from the manure process, which eventually found its way onto the mouths of many a pretty girl – in the form of lipstick! Poetic justice in the circumstances, don't you think? Often, as I contemplated what I was doing in such a meaningful and worthwhile occupation, I would ponder with no shame whatsoever the prospect of a handsome millionaire whisking me away from all of this – and fast!

The job did have its compensations, though. Not the least of these was a what-you-see-is-what-you-get type of office manager - Mr Edwards. In his gruff down-to-earth tones he would reliably inform me that 'Tha' gets best cup o' tea by warming' t'pot first afore letting it stand for five minutes after mashing.' I have to tell you that this nugget of wisdom has remained with me to this day and is followed slavishly to the letter. Vital education indeed!

I remember too, the Calder river running as a beck behind the water treatment works; and walking through the plant to the banks of the canal for my lunch – what beauty, honestly - gathering blackberries on the way and soaking them on my return, not in the beck, of course, but in the office sink! They say that what goes round comes around – and Mum proved this. She would make jam from the garnered blackberries, which was duly 'returned' by me to the office for gleeful consumption by my colleagues. As you can see, it all happened in Halifax!

My next post was as a medical records clerk at Halifax Royal Infirmary in the Accident and Emergency Department filing and drawing records of patients in addition to opening the mail and typing notes for the hospital's orthopaedic surgeons. After only a year in the post I was promoted to medical secretary looking after four consultants. To be honest, though, the medical terminology proved rather difficult for me to grasp and I soon discovered that my duties were becoming more gruelling and exacting. Rather than stay in a position I was not happy with, I decided to leave the health service altogether. I managed to secure a secretarial post at Provincial Insurance but from day one it was doomed. Working relations with my employer never really blossomed and I remember leaving rather abruptly one day following a disagreement. After this, I found temporary work as a stop-gap ahead of my chosen career path as a model and beautician.

# CHAPTER 3
# IN FRONT OF THE CAMERA

Mum must have noticed my modelling potential from an early age as she arranged my first 'shoot', by a professional snapper, a Hugh Greaves, at his business premises in King Cross. I was 18 months old!

Further sittings were arranged of me in my infant state, when, at the age of three, I was bridesmaid for my godmother, and again two years later with my favourite doll before I began at Miss Oakley's school.

Clifford Nicholl, the husband of Mum's special wartime dancing chum Kathleen, would also take snaps of me, occasionally with his daughter Susan, a school-friend of mine.

Our relationship still remains intact, although these day's we keep in touch by letter as this is the only practical way of doing so.

Sue is married to Ken Koo, a Chinese national, and the pair currently reside in Hong Kong with their two children – so I can hardly nip round for a cup of coffee!

Mr Nicholl would pass on tips on the correct way to pose and when we went on holiday, he and Dad would both be busy with their cameras taking shots of Sue and myself.

Some years later, in 1965, Diane Parker and I both attended the Louise Morton School of Beauty in Sowerby Bridge for a six-week crash course in etiquette, make up, poise, deportment and table manners after which we blossomed into models for local businesses.

But we needed to get 'noticed' and to this end, one of the foremost ways was to be photographed as often as possible. The two of us were still waiting when our fortunes changed and we had a stroke of luck – and all in the same year. For my part, after being crowned Halifax Charity Gala Queen in 1967, I was introduced to another amateur photographer, Kenneth Greenwood, by Diane at Mr Smith's Easter Bunny competition. After attending a photo shoot at Lightcliffe, Mr Greenwood later held further sessions at the Dickinson Studios in Manchester before arranging for me to appear in the audience and record a session of the hugely popular Top of the Pops programme, set to be televised in May 1969 and which would feature Lulu and Cliff Richard. Angela Hughes accompanied me for the week-end recording.

Diane then arranged for me to meet Dennis Lever, who gave me my first experiences of photographic modelling and taught me how to pose. The shoots were voluntary until I joined an agency, Demonstration Promotions of Leeds, in March 1968, where I received the princely sum of £3 an hour.

Earlier in 1967, I met up with David Glendenning from Stockport, another amateur photographer who took pictures of myself and other West Yorkshire beauty queens at a photo-shoot at what is now the Dr Bernard's children's home at Norland in Halifax.

But then, as if by magic, over the next few weeks, modelling assignments stared to flow for Diane and myself - at the Victoria Hall in Halifax, Ken Greenwood's Lightliffe home, and David Glendenning's studio in Leeds.

I have to say that Dennis Lever's contribution to my career was invaluable; he continued to 'snap' me for 19 years - a long and fruitful association in which none of his photographic advice went amiss.

It is, of course, important to all models and beauty contestants that they look their best, whether in he flesh, as it were, or in pictorial form. Dennis Lever's favourite spots for photo shoots were at Scamander Dam, Saddleworth Moors, Hinsdale sand dunes near Southport, Morecambe Bay and Blackpool seafront.

When I was taking my first beauty steps In the early days it was Mum who gave me make-up and behaviour tips. But when a fashion consultation was required, Mum turned to Auntie Doris, a dressmaker.

Between them, they helped to guide me in the right direction and their efforts, along with those of my photographic friends, began to make me feel confident that my catwalk career would have a promising start.

## CHAPTER 4
## AN EXACTING ROUTINE

At last, I now had the opportunity to do what I had always dreamed of doing and I was determined to give it my best shot – and make Mum and Dad proud of me.

Like all jobs, there is a learning curve to negotiate but I was /wise enough to know that not everything would happen at once. And so it was that I realised hard work would have to be the order of the day if I was to succeed.

Preparations for a competition would always begin the night before when I would apply three layers of QT Quick tan I applied circles, not straight lines, so the cream did not end up in streaks before retiring to bed in some old pyjamas.

Quick tans, which were usually applied the day before a contest, were legal but stockings and instant tans were not. One girl I remember paraded round a swimming pool sporting a quick tan but the weather changed; it began to rain and she took on a 'mottled' appearance as the tan had not set properly. She then resorted to an instant tan - and promptly received a ticking-off from the chaperon. For the record, she was placed fourth.

This procedure reminds me of a little story.

Getting ready the following morning began in earnest at eight o'clock as I first put up my heated rollers, covering them with a headscarf before asking Dad to take me to the station to catch the train for either Blackpool to enter a Miss United Kingdom heat, or Morecambe for a Miss Great Britain heat contest.

The train usually left at nine o'clock, make-up being applied during the journey. I would change trains at either Preston or Liverpool and meet other contestants along the way.

If I saw my friend June Wilkinson from Leeds, we would discuss girly things, such as letters from admirers and some of the weird requests they made, like drinking champagne out of our shoes, or asking for a lock of our hair. We did not reply to most of these letters because we saw them as just a source of amusement.

Arriving at the venue at one o'clock, I would invariably meet Barbara Ponsford, whose husband owned a furniture company in Sheffield, and she would usually be at the mirror combing her long blonde locks. Barbara would greet me with, "Hello Jan, how are you? Come and join us," beckoning me towards the mirror. "Put your bag down here next to me, I'll see it's safe. Join me when you've changed."

I would then leave her to change into my swimsuit before rejoining her to arrange my hair from curlers to ringlets. I would do the front and she would dress out the back before I checked my hair in a mirror.

Then, Barbara Garvey, from Poulton-le-Fylde, would walk into the dressing room and discuss with Diane the show fortunes of their respective dogs. Juggling breeding poodles with a part-time business clipping all breeds at her clients' homes was just the ticket for 'Barbara G'.

This sort of banter was normal practice only between the regular contestants but I was lucky to have been introduced to the other girls by Diane Parker the first time I appeared on the beauty circuit (at a heat of Miss England at Wakefield Tiffany's in 1967), otherwise I would have been kept at 'arms length' until I had made a few more contest appearances.

As you will no doubt appreciate, there was plenty of preparatory work to engage in before stepping up the catwalk.

My routine consisted of firstly applying Optrex eye lotion, cleanser, toner and moisturizer together in upward and downward movements across the face.

Four upward strokes to neck area and three upward strokes to the cheeks followed before continuing with five strokes upwards to the forehead and, finally, three downward strokes to the nose and chin.

In those days, Optrex was acceptable but nowadays it is not recommended due to an ingredient which brings the pupils forward. I only used a mild rosewater toner but other strong ones had a drying effect and yet stronger ones would even remove the top layer of skin. The effect of the toner could be put back by applying two layers of moisturiser before massaging well with upward movements of the fingers.

Back on the circuit, at one o'clock, the organisers of the competition would join us and ask us to fill in the entry forms prior to all of us being asked to stand in line to receive our numbers. At two o'clock the contest would commence with a walk around the swimming pool in numerical order. The judges were placed at the far side of the pool and to get to them we had to walk a very long way, often with a dry mouth due to nerves - and with only a polo mint to quench the thirst.

Singers, dancers and several other performers are frequently reminded to show 'eyes and teeth' when strutting their stuff on stage – and we were no different: after all, there is nothing worse than a glum beauty contestant.

We were told to smile pleasantly and look appealing to the press and public photographers, who would often ask us to pose along the way.

Having completed one circuit, we would walk in front of the judges twice more to give them every opportunity to make up their minds as to who were going to be the lucky girl to win that day.

The decision made, and after the customary tense wait, the winner would then be presented with the usual cash prize of ten pounds - and a place in the final.

# CHAPTER 5
# A YEAR TO REMEMBER

In 1966, following England's triumph in the World Cup, I was honoured to be chosen to represent my hometown after winning my local heat of the Miss Yorkshire Young Conservative personality contest.

I could hardly believe it but Lady Luck favoured me on this occasion as I was selected first in the heat giving me an automatic ticket to the Harrogate final. Unfortunately, I failed to impress the judges with my political knowledge in the north Yorkshire town – unlike the winner, a lady from Leeds, who, to be fair, thoroughly deserved her success.

It is perhaps worth pointing out that the Halifax heats for Miss Yorkshire Young Conservative were held in February each year, this contest always attracting a great deal of interest.

For my own part, and whilst being a member of the King Cross branch of the Young Conservatives, I was fortunate enough to be selected to represent my local division when I won the heat at the age of 19 – my very first success on the catwalk.

The fact that I missed out in the Harrogate final to a Leeds girl mattered little to me – I had arrived!

So pleased was I with my initial triumph that I informed Halifax Courier readers that it was the local Young Conservatives who 'fanned the flames' for me as far as beauty competitions were concerned; they persuaded me it would provide good publicity for the party!

Later, I paid a visit to Diane after the Miss Young Conservative heat to listen to more advice as you could never honestly say you knew everything.

Our respective mothers were in the Halifax Women's Institute Choir, who attended rehearsals at Crossley & Porter school on Wednesday evenings. Following one such rehersal Diane's Mum introduced us at their home and we have maintained our close friendship ever since. Bosom buddies, if ever there were two!

Diane first introduced me to the bona fide beauty circuit in March, 1967 when she took me to a Miss England heat at Wakefield one Wednesday evening. I was naturally very excited – and very nervous but It proved to be a successful venture for both Diane and myself as I claimed second spot whilst Diane was placed third.

We prepared ourselves for the contest in the 'boudoir', a dressing– room adjoining the ladies' toilet!

Arriving at seven to be ready for the first swimsuit parade at eight, I already had my hair in curlers and my make-up applied, which only left eye-shadow, mascara, rouge and lipstick to be put in place – before combing and brushing my hair out of curlers and into ringlets, which happened to be the style of the day.

Our next port of call was York Tiffany's, where in a Miss England heat, Diane scooped the main honour whilst I was awarded the runner-up prize.

But with hardly any opportunity to draw breath, I was back on the road again, travelling to Stockton-on-Tees with Diane to appear in a heat of the Miss Fiesta competition.

But I could not help feeling guilty as the events of the evening unfolded. Diane had driven to around 90 miles to Teesside, helped me with my make-up preparations, corrected my hairstyle and advised me on the costume I was going to wear for the heat.

Imagine how I felt, therefore, when that doyen of entertainers, Bruce Forsyth, announced me as the winner. Diane had done so much for me but, unfortunately, this time she did not even make it to the short-list. However, she achieved success in a later heat of the same contest – and duly went forward to the final at the Fiesta Club in Sheffield. But Fate conspired against both of us and we returned home empty-handed.

Success and failure are strange bedfellows as I was discovering. But after a setback, all the girls quickly adopted the grin–and-bear-it attitude, took the defeats and prepared for the next contest. We couldn't, and didn't, lose them all!

So, on with the motley; the Jersey Holiday Queen heat in Leeds followed soon after, Diane taking the winners sash whilst I was placed second.

I was beginning to enjoy life in the 'swinging' Sixties; it was an interesting time to be young, to say the least – and all seemed right with the world.

Meanwhile, these were the days when the country was in the midst of 'flower power'; **The Beatles** had launched *Sergeant Pepper* and **Procul Harum** was topping the pop charts with *'A Whiter Shade of Pale'*.

Elsewhere, on the beauty circuit, scores of young hopefuls had the whole country to compete in as there were no mileage restrictions with regard to entering contests.

But for a less than seasoned campaigner on the beauty circuit, it was a hectic period as I darted from contest to contest in pursuit of fame at best – and recognition at least.

And it was in 1967 that Diane and I had our photographs taken by the one and only David Bailey, who was then a trainee snapper working for the Daily Mirror. Heady stuff indeed, for a mere secretary!

Later that year in May I took part in the Halifax Charity Gala Queen contest along with my school friend Angela Hughes. She suggested we enter the competition because a holiday in Italy was the top prize – an opportunity too good to miss, we thought.

We duly sent off the entry forms and could not believe our luck when we received an invitation to attend the first stage of the competition at Spring Hall, Manor Heath in the town.

The 60 contestants were finally reduced to 13 semi-finalists – with the two of us amongst them.

We were each placed amongst the lucky 13, who were all asked to return to Spring Hall later the same week when the judges would make their final decision.

On that night, Angela and I were both apprehensive as we were interviewed again – this time in front of six local councillors.

In the event 13 became six as fellow contestants Marilyn O'Connor, Rhonda Guillot, Rosalinde Hey, Margaret Whitehouse, Jean Sutcliffe and myself – but sadly, no Angela - were selected to attend the final at the Alexandra Hall in Halifax on a Saturday evening in May. The three judges officiating that night were the well-known Sixties pop star Billy J. Kramer, John Pickles, chairman of the Gala Committee and Miss Beryl Whitaker, whose firm had sponsored the holiday prize.

Billy J. and his band, the Dakotas, entertained the audience before Mr Pickles announced the result we had been waiting for. I could not believe my luck as the names were read out in reverse order – with my name last! I had won the marvellous Italian holiday – and spending money, too!

After this success, the Halifax Courier published an article about me passing beauty secrets onto budding catwalk queens.

The competition heats began each year in May with the finals held in early June although the Halifax Gala itself took place during Wakes Week in late July when the town closed down completely.

It certainly is a special occasion in the community, especially as all businesses took their holidays around the day of the carnival with the exception of the Playhouse theatre and the Halifax Evening Courier.

And so I went to my friend Diane who gave me some valuable advice on beauty tips - including how to 'brown' the body (by using the contents of the whole bottle!) - and detailing methods of co-ordinating make-up and clothes. "I'm not a professional by any means," I told the paper. "It's just another hobby for me – but a very expensive one!"

The article also included comments on the so-called 'admirers' who followed contestants around the circuit. Some of these would even write letters asking for locks of my hair, or one of my shoes from which to drink champagne to toast my happiness – truly! Thankfully, in general, the sentiments people expressed about beauty queens in those days were very encouraging with comments mainly turning out to be harmless sources of fun.

All of us on the circuit, however, knew that complacency was a curse. Whilst delighted to have been chosen as Halifax Charity Gala Queen, for example, there were other competitions still to enter – and therefore resting on one's laurels was not an option!

So it was that on the Tuesday following the Halifax event I found myself, along with Diane, in a heat of Southport's English Rose contest.

Barbara Garvey and I were later chosen as reserves to Carol Cawood and Elizabeth Lamb – and for our efforts were presented with a set of six guest towels!  How are the mighty fallen?

The next day, however, I was fortunate enough to be selected and added to the list of 11 girls to go forward to the finals of the Miss Great Britain competition which were to be held at Morecambe in September.

The beauty circuit had plenty to offer if its many aspirants were willing to travel around as Diane and I were prepared to do. We proved this when we entered the Miss Cleethorpes competition, where the heats and final were all held one Saturday evening at the end of the pier. On that night, Diane won, whilst I took the runners-up sash - and the bottles of Dubonnet and sherry we respectively received went down very nicely indeed!

In the Sixties, beauty queens were regarded as celebrities and were often asked to judge contests themselves – and Diane Parker fell into that category.

She was invited to join Bob Monkhouse, Pete Murray, Douglas 'Cardew' Robinson and Sean Connery in Norwich to help select Miss Anglia Television, 1967.

I later followed in her footsteps, in a smaller way, by judging a heat of Miss England at Tiffany's in Sheffield in two years' later.

However, in October 1967, whilst working for the Sir Lindsay Parkinson construction company on the Boothwood Dam project as a secretary/ receptionist, I entered, as Halifax Charity Gala Queen, the competition for the National Carnival Queen of the United Kingdom, the final of which was held at Shrewsbury.

The earlier semi-finals had been held at Crewe, where 75 contestants – all beauty queens in their own right - had been reduced to 35 for the short trip to Shropshire. I remember the nervous tension I experienced as 35 girls waited to hear whether they had made it to the next stage. Delighted at being selected in the 12 to go through to the penultimate stage, I nevertheless was resigned to my fate at being so near and yet so far once again. Or so I thought. But I was in for a very pleasant surprise as the names of the final five contestants were announced - and mine was one of them. After another long wait, the torment was over as the three judges had, at last, made their decisions.

You can imagine my feelings as the compere read out my name last of all. I was over the moon – and completely 'lost it'. So pleased was I at scooping a top title that I burst into tears, grabbed the runner-up, and squeezed the hand of my predecessor in a vice-like grip. Success! For the record, my prize for winning that evening was my first national title, £20, together with expenses for any engagements attended during the following 12 months.

1967 was turning out to be both an exciting and exhausting year - but I was certainly enjoying it.

Contacts were now coming thick and fast but the adrenalin continued to flow and when that happened, it was important to stay with the action.

I shall always remember the Halifax Gala Day when I rode on a float in the Charity Gala Parade.  On a glorious June day, the sun was shining from a cloudless sky as we paraded through the town before arriving at Manor Heath where the entertainment included acrobats, weightlifters, muscle men, balloon-blowers, milk-drinkers, and chimpanzees from Flamingo Park helping to create all the fun of the fair.

I recall that one of my duties on the day was to pose with a group of chimpanzees. Highly mischievous, they pulled my hair and tugged my sash. And it was very hard to keep them still for the photo call but all went well in the end – eventually!

It was a particular pleasure to represent my home town and I felt a great sense of pride in doing so, especially as many of my responsibilities were new experiences for me.

Not least of these I remember was a visit to the Olympic Health Studios where I was introduced to the proprietor, Dennis Linford, and some of the hopefuls for the Mr Halifax competition. Men can look good too – and, as I recall, one or two of them certainly did!

One of the joys in competing at summer resorts was the chance to meet the stars of stage, screen and television. And such an event occurred when I entered the seventh heat of the Miss Blackpool bathing beauty competition where my favourite comedian in those days - Hugh Lloyd of Hancock's Half Hour fame – was one of the judges. He placed me third in the seventh heat and to this day I still have the envelope with his marks on the back as a memento of the occasion.

In a later heat of the same competition held at the Grafton Rooms in

Liverpool, I managed to claim the runners-up spot. But as only winners progressed to the final of Miss United Kingdom, I was once again thwarted. In the last week of August, Diane suggested we both should enter the Queen of Queens' competition to be held at the Lucas Show Ground, Oldham. Here, I was placed fourth and was delighted when I learnt that my portrait was to be painted by a local artist.

As a point of interest, when attending national competition heats, especially at Blackpool and Morecambe, I would be halfway round the pool and find my mouth becoming dry through nervousness. I would reach into my cleavage where I had usually secreted two polo mints - and in the cover of the diving boards I would place a mint in my mouth. This gave me the confidence to return to the parade with the required 'air'.

The beauty business is full of ups and downs and so it proved after Dennis Lever submitted my picture for the photographic heat of Miss Sunday Mirror. I was subsequently asked to attend the live Blackpool heat in July where I was placed fourth to qualify for the final which was to be held two months later, but the stiff competition meant I would only reach the 12-strong short-list.

However, I began to realise that if I was going to be successful I had to persevere. And so naturally, I was delighted when, at the Clearasil Teen Queen contest, I was rewarded with the first prize - and a place in the national final in London on New Year's Eve, where I again reached the final dozen on the short-list.

Progressing no further in that particular competition, I could not help wondering what the New Year would bring. After all, I was only 21 but ambitious enough to want to continue in the business. A change in fortune in the following twelve months, therefore, was awaited with some eagerness.

# CHAPTER 6
# SUCCESS!

My parents announced my engagement to Andrew in 1967, and I decided he would accompany me on a trip to Italy. I had been crowned Halifax Gala Queen and this was may prize which needed to be used! We received the star treatment as we were interviewed and photographed at Leeds Bradford airport before boarding the plane for the Adriatic resort of Cattolica.

Although we departed on a short holiday, I could not escape work entirely, as after a few days of very pleasant sunbathing I had to abandon the beach for my only public engagement.

As part of my Gala Queen duties, I had to judge a local heat of the Miss Italy competition. It was an honour and I was delighted to take part.

During the second week Andrew and I left Cattolica for three days in Rome, two in Florence and one in Verona before returning home.

I had not been back many days when my agency, Demonstration Promotions of Leeds, gave me a chance to work for local fashion couturier, Sophisti-Kat, modelling swimwear.

Dennis Lever set up the photographic shoot as he had done when giving me my first chance on the road to stardom.

My next venue with Dennis was at Crossley and Porter School, a beautiful building of Victorian architecture erected by the Crossley family, who I had always admired and studied in my school projects. I had longed to enter these magnificent premises, which in those days were a male domain only. The manager of Jack Lee's swimwear and sports products asked if I knew any males who could model trunks and wetsuits. I suggested Andrew as a possible candidate because I thought he would be delighted with the extra money as he was still studying. Reluctantly, he managed to put in an appearance for one show only – his masculine pride forbidding any further performances!

In September, I took my place in the final of the Southport English Rose contest, Dennis Lever and my parents attending as well to give welcome support. However, I was not selected amongst the winners on this occasion, and returned home empty-handed.

Throughout my career on the catwalk I never used to wish I was more beautiful than other girls. What concerned me more was whether or not I had chosen the correct dress for the competitions I had entered as it was vital I remained 'a dedicated follower of fashion' at all times.

Undaunted, therefore, I pressed on as it was important for me to continue in my quest. I was young, impressionable, full of determination to succeed and grateful for my Mum's advice on the matter. "Go forward with confidence with the Lord at your back," she would say. Wise words, indeed, which helped me a lot.

Suitably encouraged, I decided that during the autumn and winter months, nightclubs would become beauty venues for me. I can safely say I am no stranger to the likes of Batley Variety Club, Manchester's Ritz, and Sheffield's Fiesta Club.

Really, though, success is never far away and I was soon on the road again, claiming a heat of Miss England at Sheffield Tiffany's.

I was pleased my friend Diane and I would compete against each other in the final phase of the prestigious competition, but Fate decreed the two of us would only reach the last 18.

Hoping for greater success in 1968 Diane and myself, along with our friends Christine Clements and Barbara Bloor, made our way to the Miss Gala Cavalcade contest held at the Owlerton Stadium, Sheffield in April - but it was not to be for any of us.

Once again, failure reared its ugly head. But there was always hope for success on the horizon. We all had to believe our respective fortunes would change. And for some of us, they did.

In June, however, our fortunes certainly did change when our foursome attended a heat of Miss Great Britain at Morecambe and I was lucky enough to be placed third, one of the judges that night being television actor Raymond Francis – Inspector Lockhart of 'No Hiding Place' fame.  I had a problem, though, when the hostess Miss Fisher said my swimsuit was too revealing and promptly placed a rose down my cleavage!

Afterwards we all dined at a local restaurant, as was our custom, after the competition, we called this the winners treat. We discussed the events of the day – laughing and saying philosophically: "We just take turns at winning!"

Getting to contest venues was done by car - or train occasionally - Diane usually sharing the driving with Pam Wood as we travelled the highways and byways of England and Wales.

Four girls – Pam, Diane, Barbara Ponsford and myself - journeying together, sharing experiences with curlers in hair under headscarves - applying the 'tutty' (make-up) as we went. We all had the same passion, in those days, and so the excitement and expectation of winning a heat or a final is easy to imagine. At other times, my parents and Andrew would accompany me, Dad remarking: "A little bit of powder, a little bit of paint, makes a girl just what she ain't." but I hope he didn't really mean that.

I remember making a conscious decision to try my luck in the Miss New Brighton competition, the plan being to use this contest as well as the Miss Great Britain at Morecambe - on alternate Wednesdays - until I won!

I had no success in the Miss Blackpool contest either but an intrepid Daily Mail reporter, Carol Lee, after trying her luck and wrote a splendid article about her experience as a beauty contestant.

She described how she had to learn to walk in order to gain the right stance so the judges could get the perfect view of all her attributes (!) while completing the quarter mile lap around the open-air swimming pool - and entitled her article, 'How I learned to walk with a ha'penny on my navel'.

Carol acquired a new swimsuit, tan make-up, stiletto-heeled shoes and a trip to the hairdresser's before entering the contest. She also stressed how amazed she was that all the girls were so friendly, with no catty tricks in evidence and she also described the marvellous encouragement the spectators gave her and the other contestants.

In truth, the 'ordeal' was over before she realised it, she wrote. It was however, an experience she would always remember. But for the rest of us there was still much more travelling to be done.

During the first week of October, I entered the Jersey Holiday Queen contest at the Locarno ballroom in Leeds winning my heat and going forward to the final, due to take place on the island the following May. Three friends – June Wilkinson, Maureen Gibbons and Audrey Hall – were also successful at the October event and we were all presented with tickets for a long weekend for two.

Later the same month my Bradford agency offered me a week's catwalk modelling at the Motor Show and Boat Show in Leeds and London during April and November the following year.

Work continued throughout the winter months as June Wilkinson and I decided to travel to Leeds, Sheffield, Doncaster, Hull, Newcastle and Sunderland to promote Players Number Six cigarettes during the daytime. For these promotions, June and I each wore a white blouse and turquoise mini-skirt with a white sash displaying 'Players Number Six' in turquoise lettering – and white 'boots'. At first, we were employed in the larger outlets including Woolworths, Binns and Hodgson & Hepworths before moving to smaller concerns such as local newsagents. But by night, wearing turquoise and silver lamè cat-suits, the pair of us would be found promoting the famous Nottingham 'gaspers' at Batley Variety Club, Tiffany's (in Leeds and Bradford) and the Fiesta Club in Stockport.

All this was grist to the mill, though; you took what you could – within reason - and were grateful.

In fact, many girls in those days and later, could also lay claim to having worn Players' famous white sash - Joy Adams, Janet Withey and Wendy George being three who spring readily to mind. But the irony was that, as beauty contestants, none of us were allowed to smoke!

It was after finishing a promotion at Hodgson & Hepworths' store in Doncaster that I remember casually remarking to my mother: 'I would like to live there someday' - never dreaming that this wish would come to fruition a few years later.

Things did not always go according to plan on the beauty circuit, of course. At a heat of Southport's English Rose competition I was feeling very content; I was doing what I really wanted and enjoying every minute of it. Then, in the middle of the afternoon as I paraded around the swimming pool, I developed a pain in my side. At the time, I thought it was a nasty attack of stitch but later, whilst on the second circuit of the pool, the discomfort persisted and would not disappear – even after taking a 'magic' polo mint! I managed to smile through the contest and survive enough to win through with Gaynor Lacey, saying: "Come on Janet, don't fail me, smile, I do believe we can win this one." And, she was right - our luck was in.  We were selected joint winners of what was the last heat – in August - before the final the following month.

On returning home after the contest I informed Mum of my discomfort, and she suggested a check up with my doctor. He diagnosed a grumbling appendix - and these attacks would continue at intervals for a further two years.

For the Southport contest, two girls were chosen each week and both were presented with a hairdressing voucher and an Eros swimming costume to wear in the final.

At the final itself, Dennis Lever was again busy recording every moment of the occasion from the point I arrived at the Lancashire resort.

He took pictures of me in my everyday dress and I can recall a visit to Andre Bernard's for facial, manicure and hairdressing before he finally snapped me in line-ups of evening dress and swimsuit.

In the end, it seemed a pity I was not selected, as he had gone to so much trouble.

However, disappointment was never far away for all of us but the answer was always to hold onto hope and keep a positive attitude.

In between contests, we had to maintain an active lifestyle by working at all manner of jobs. Some, though, were better than others.

Whilst working temporarily at Hoffman's Garage in Halifax, I was asked to help them with publicity. This included a trip round the town, accompanied on the journey by two other staff members, Miss Muriel Shorrocks and Mr Howard the chauffeur. We rode in a Rolls-Royce Silver Ghost Roi de Beiges tourer, which had just competed in the London to Edinburgh veteran car rally. The beautiful limousine, built by Woodall Nicholson, of Well Lane, Halifax in 1913, originally cost £600 and had once transported Prime Minister Stanley Baldwin to a whole host of venues nationwide.

What a life! And as someone once famously remarked: 'You can't lose them all.'

During a long weekend away from my secretarial duties at Hoffman's I took my place on the catwalk again in the March final of Miss Britain where I managed to reach the last 18 before being eliminated.

Later in the year, whilst working for Webster's Brewery in Halifax, I entered an evening heat of Miss England at the Manchester Ritz and was awarded the third prize.

On the circuit, it was important to take whatever award was available as it would have been all too easy to enter 'selected' events in the hope of changing one's fortune. In truth, it was a case of 'the more, the merrier'.

If a competition was being staged anywhere, it was seen as vital that we should be there – provided we were fit in wind and limb!

Before we could barely turn round, the finals of Miss United Kingdom were upon us and so Diane, June and I, ever faithful to the cause, took the Pullman from Leeds to London to take part in the prestigious competition. Unfortunately, on this occasion, although we made the last 18, that was as far as we got.

Disappointed but not dismayed, June and I hit the catwalk soon after at the fourth heat of Miss Batley Variety Club, where I was placed second, June coming third, behind newcomer Lynn Windsor.

Earlier in the year, I had been lucky enough to be selected from 35 other contestants - all carnival queens representing their hometowns – to be handed the title of National Carnival Queen in Shrewsbury - and a prize of £20, a crown, sash, and a cup to be held for a year. Perhaps it was fortunate I was wearing my lucky purple Lurex mini dress!

One of my many duties as carnival queen in my hometown was riding through the streets in an open-topped BMW sports car in places as far away Crewe and Nantwich in Cheshire, waving to the public in carnival parades. Heady stuff - but enjoyable for all that.

In those days I used to earn £3 a day from modelling but for the 'Halifax' appearances, expenses were the norm.

One September evening at the Alexandra Hall in Halifax, I handed my Charity Gala Queen title over to Wendy Atkinson, who had been selected as the 1968 winner.

After the contest, Wendy asked what her duties as Charity Gala Queen might be and I gladly took the opportunity to reminisce, informing her that I had pushed over tall towers of pennies before helping to count them for charity. Walking ten miles to raise money for a cerebral palsy unit at the Royal Halifax Infirmary, now known as the Milner Wing. These tasks she could be expected to perform for a small charge of only expenses.

During the first week of October, I entered the Jersey Holiday Queen competition and won my heat securing a place in the final in May 1969.

Three of my friends, June Wilkinson, Maureen Gibbons and Audrey Hall, were also selected and we were all presented with

tickets for a long weekend for two in addition to some spending money.

During December, my agency once again asked me to sell Lego sets at Redgates in Sheffield; a very interesting promotion as I had never experienced working with children before.

However, difficulties arose when I had to hide presents for parents to collect later on so the myth of Father Christmas could be kept alive. Nine times out of ten the little darlings did not see the presents, which were hidden under the table, waiting to be taken to the stock room for wrapping ready for collection by their parents before they left the store!

# CHAPTER 7
# RULES OF ENGAGEMENT

Competing in various parts of the country was fun – irksome occasionally - but fun all the same.

However, what we all had to do was not just confined to turning up at venues and smiling sweetly whilst walking around a bathing pool.

It was vital that each girl knew the rules of every competition she was entering – and there were many!

Contestants for Miss United Kingdom, Miss England and Miss Britain had to be aged between 18 and 26 – and those between 18 and 21 had to have the signatures of their parents or guardians before being allowed to take part. Elsewhere, at Butlin's, for example, any girl over 16 could enter, while 15 was the minimum age at Pontin's.

In addition, the costumes worn by the girls in pursuit of the various titles had to conform to exact requirements: there was no place for any apparel which could be termed risqué or which might offend common decency. Depending on personal points of view, though, the Miss Blackpool contest was the only one in which girls could wear bikinis!

All competitions in the Sixties and Seventies were judged on charm, personality and poise, and the daywear, swimwear and evening wear in which we paraded had to reflect these qualities. Judging panels were sometimes split in finals with three judges voting for one contestant and the other three for another, usually the chairman of the judges, having the casting vote if necessary.

For the record, only swimsuits were worn in the heats of the national contests, including those for Miss Great Britain, whereas for Miss New Brighton – a different type of competition altogether - there were separate fashion and swimwear contests. Entrants were also chaperoned for heats and finals of the Miss Great Britain and Miss UK contests. Indeed, many of my contemporaries will well remember Miss Fisher (at Miss Great Britain) and the redoubtable Miss Julia Morley, wife of the celebrated 'In Reverse Order' Eric – more of whom later - who kept the girls on the straight and narrow path at all the major contests the Mecca organisation ran.

Indeed, I remember clearly the unforgettable Eric was very vigilant at rehearsals of Miss England 1968 making sure all the contestants knew exactly where we were going and what we were doing whilst appearing in the three consecutive categories of evening dress, day dress and swimwear. At what could be three rehearsals in total, he was particular as to where we all stood, which was usually half way down the catwalk. We would pause, count for five seconds, and then pause at the end of the catwalk for a further 10 seconds.

He then chose three girls at random - I was one he 'selected' that year –
before telling us we had to pretend that we had won and that the cameras were
focused on us. Mr Morley then told us to pause at the winning podium for 30
seconds before taking an extra 10 seconds at the end of each of the three
catwalks. A series of manoeuvres later, all 75 of us finished up standing along
the three catwalks before the final 18 girls were chosen. This was especially
nerve-racking and I can remember thinking that training as an actress would
have been useful to carry it out. But we all took a deep breath, swallowed hard
and hoped our nerves would hold long enough for us to get through this
ordeal.

Also for the contest, we had to wear the same style of swimming costume; a
navy blue one-piece with a diagonal white stripe, which sported a gold star on
the right-hand side.  In addition, all contestants wore similar-style evening
dresses at the beginning of the parade and we were only allowed to change into
a cocktail dress if we reached the last 18 at the close of the swimwear section
– which Diane and I were lucky enough to do on this occasion.

The two of us, shared a room at the Waldorf hotel for the duration of the
competition held in London, but we were not fully prepared we had not
brought our cocktail dresses with us when we travelled south on the Pullman
train. We were, therefore, somewhat taken aback when Julia Morley, who had
herself been a beauty queen, invited the pair of us to accompany her on a
shopping trip to Regent Street to purchase the required cocktail dresses. She

had suggested that we 'may be chosen to appear in the last 18' and would therefore need cocktail dresses. We were - and we did! Although it should be said for the record the last 18 was as far as we got, as, for the record, Yvette Livesey took the title.

Our fair but firm dominatrix Mrs Morley completely took over our lives – for three hours at least – as we glided through a series of boutiques and gown outlets in the West End in a bid to secure the dresses. In the event, I selected a purple lurex mini-dress whilst Diane chose a pink and white balloon-style creation. Suitably clad – and three hours later - the three of us took the relatively short journey back to the Waldorf in time for dinner prior to rehearsal that evening.

As with all the top competitions, rehearsals were of vital importance, especially when proceedings were televised, such as Miss England 1968, for example.

The contests, although glamorous, were often arduous with rehearsals and meals in quick succession over a three-day period. Standing around posing and posturing whilst grinning through clenched teeth was not always easy to do and not every girl was in the right frame of mind to undertake such tasks. However, the golden pot at the end of the rainbow served to focus our minds as we never knew who would or would not be successful on the night – and that fact provided the adrenalin rush for all of us.

Mecca, which ran the Miss UK, Miss England, Miss Britain, Miss World and from 2000, Miss Earth contests, would not knowingly allow married women to take part whereas Rank, who operated the Miss Great Britain and Miss Universe competitions, certainly did.

But the list of unacceptable items went on and included such gems as no tights, no stockings, no extra internal padding of swimsuits and no false hair. But several of the girls often got away with a little 'manipulation' in regard to the last two of these.

There was to be no application of 'allegedly' false tan either - although there was - occasionally!

Furthermore, contestants could travel from anywhere in the country in those days, unlike today when only a 30-mile radius is allowed. In my day, there were no mobile phones, so it could be argued that girls are able to move around in a safer environment today than was the case 30 years ago.

In spite of the changing times, however, everyone loves to see a pretty girl – a fact that doesn't change – and that is the reason beauty pageants are here to stay!

Photographic contests such as Miss Variety Club of Great Britain, Miss Daily Mirror, Miss Sunday Mirror, Miss Vegetarian, and Miss Ambre Solaire were different in that twenty girls were selected for each of the local heats; Miss North – South – East and West prior to a final individual appearance where a winner would be chosen.

Nobody knew where or who was to be chosen until your letter came to tell you where to be and at what time. We all used to wait eagerly for these letters and thought it a great honour to be chosen from all of Britain's beauties. We would all happily read the letters before congratulating each other on our success. On the evening of the heat (really like a semi-final) four girls would be selected from each heat to attend a national final.

# CHAPTER 8
# YESTERDAY AND TODAY

Historically, beauty contests were introduced to British culture relatively recently - straight after World War Two, in fact.

Seaside resorts throughout England, including Eastbourne, Great Yarmouth, Weston-super-Mare, Skegness and Cleethorpes staged competitions on a regular basis following the ceasing of hostilities but the greatest enthusiasm for seeing young ladies parading in bathing costumes in particular, could be found in the Lancashire resorts of Morecambe, New Brighton, Southport and Blackpool.

In Morecambe, for example, where I enjoyed competing once every three weeks during the season, the new swimming stadium became the venue for holidaymakers and day-trippers alike would flock there on Wednesday afternoons to gaze at fresh-faced 16 to 20 - somethings walking slowly around the magnificent pool before being 'placed' by a select panel of judges.

After starting out in 1946 as the Bathing Beauty Queen, the Morecambe competition, organised by the local council, progressed to the grander title of Miss Great Britain some years later.

For the record, a teenage civil servant, Lydia Reid - from Morecambe - was the first winner and collected a cup, seven guineas and a swimsuit for her troubles. And to think she did all this in a downpour in front of over 4,000 people who were soaked to the skin! That's dedication for you.

But Morecambe and Heysham Council had a rush of blood the following year and increased the prize money to £100. They kept on increasing it over the years so that by the Fifties, when beauty contests were mainly swimsuit affairs, it had reached £1000. With this in mind, I only hope Lydia invested her seven guineas wisely!

It was not long before the Miss Great Britain competition became the contest of choice, offering, as it did, the largest cash award for any event run by a local authority. But by the time I came onto the circuit in 1967, the situation had improved dramatically, the reward for winning having risen to a mind-boggling £3,000!

Prospects got even better for the girls who scooped the accolade of Miss Great Britain as winning the prestigious prize gave them automatic entry into the Miss Universe pageant, arranged by the Rank Organisation. The Morecambe event soon set the standard for all the others to follow in what was to become an integral part of the British summer scene in the Sixties, Seventies and Eighties.

Increased prosperity in the Fifties and Sixties saw holidaymakers making journeys to coastal resorts, each one of which were in competition to attract as many people as possible to their respective hotels and guest houses. But with British travellers becoming more adventurous in the Seventies, this led

to more and more of them venturing abroad in search of guaranteed sunshine

– and in such places as the Spanish Costas, male holidaymakers especially,

had only to take a trip down to the beach to see their very own 'ready-made'

beauties, so to speak!

However, along with changing vacation habits, the Miss Great Britain contest

also altered with the times, television having a huge impact. Since 1971, the

competition's Grand Final has been staged in three parts with swimwear,

daywear and eveningwear categories filmed at three separate venues in and

around Morecambe.

In the Eighties, the public soon began to demonstrate more 'sophisticated'

tastes in holiday entertainment added to which, young women were being

offered greater career options in the wider workplace. Indeed, the contests

held at Great Yarmouth, Morecambe and Rhyl ceased in that decade - albeit

in a less dramatic fashion than those held at New Brighton, where the Wirral

resort's swimming pool was destroyed by a winter storm!

Moreover, interest among aspiring entrants waned, and fewer holidaymakers

wanted to watch the parades. Consequently, only the Miss Blackpool event,

which amended its format from afternoon swimwear to evening club-wear,

managed to survive the 'new culture', whereas the Miss Fleetwood contest

became the only 'traditional' beauty competition to make it into the new

century.

Today, I believe, the Rank organisation runs the Miss Great Britain contest formerly operated by Morecambe and Heysham Borough Council with the winners assuming automatic entry to Miss Universe and Miss Tourism.

But digressing briefly, for the record, winners of the Miss England, Miss Scotland and Miss Wales titles went forward to compete in the Miss United Kingdom competition, under the control of the Mecca Organisation – and the celebrated Morleys.

Success in taking the nation's sash and crown at the prestigious contest also meant automatic entry to the Miss World final, which, in my day, was held in early November at the Aldwych Theatre in London.

But, returning to Miss Great Britain, perhaps in an effort to keep the 'unsuccessful' finalists happy, a second bite of the cherry is nowadays available to them by way of entry into such oddly-named offshoots as Model of the World, Miss Bikini, Miss Millionaire and Miss Internet.

Oh, to have my turn again! Not really though, because I have no regrets about the years I trod the catwalk.

# CHAPTER 9
# THE MAGNIFICENT MORLEYS

No mention of the beauty business would be complete without reference to Douglas Eric Morley, sometimes known affectionately as Mr World.

He was born during the First World War in Holborn, London, his father having died when he was a baby, whilst his mother and step-father both died of tuberculosis when Eric was 11 years old.

In his early teens, Eric was sent by the then London County Council to a Royal Navy training ship, later becoming a band-boy in the Royal Fusiliers where he learnt to play the French horn. During the war, as an Army captain, he organised concerts for the troops and on demobilisation, he returned to Civvy Street in 1946 as a publicity sales manager before ultimately becoming a successful entrepreneur, creating 'Come Dancing', which went onto achieve great success as the world's longest- running television programme in those days. Later, he began to adapt traditional seaside beauty contests into fashion shows, and used them to help publicise the Festival of Britain in 1951.

The following year, Miss Universe was launched in the United States but this gave the patriotic Eric the incentive to pull out all the stops to establish the Miss World contest over here with what became an annual event held at the

Royal Albert Hall in London.

The importance of Eric Morley's role at Mecca grew rapidly and by 1953 he became a director of its dancing division.

Six years later, Miss World was first televised, and at its peak in 1966, the show received an audience

of 27.5 million in Britain alone. Although the contest is no longer broadcast in Britain on terrestrial television, it remains popular elsewhere and in 1997 attracted a worldwide audience of 2.5 million people from 155 countries.

Eric Morley also took Mecca into other directions, including the introduction of betting and gaming,

with the arrival of bingo in Britain in 1961. But such was his enterprise and dynamism that away from the glamour of the beauty pageants, he still had the energy to run 100 dance halls and 700 betting shops.

He met former beauty queen Julia Prichard in a dance hall – where else? – where she was working behind the bar, the couple tying the knot in 1960. Eric, who became Mecca chairman in 1971, had always been synonymous with the Miss World competition which is now well over 50 years old. But despite receiving its fair share of criticism, it still retains a mystique, a unique insight into the way women's lives have changed over the past half-century.

Like many girls, I was ordered about by Mr Morley at the Miss England and Miss Britain contests in 1968 and I have to confess that I would have liked to have answered back. However, I know that if I had done, I would have been 'asked to leave the stage'. But he put his heart and soul into what he was doing and had to be respected for that.

They say the end justifies the means and this was certainly the case when Eric was around because any contests he was involved with were meticulously organised and ran like clockwork, give or take the odd hitch. And therefore it was as a mark of respect to him that when he died of a heart attack some years ago, 20 former Miss Worlds attended his funeral. Ensuring that the proud tradition continued, Eric's widow Julia has expanded the Miss World organisation to embrace the internet. Satellite television rights have been sold around the world to such an extent that something in the region of two billion people will apparently soon have access to the pageant. And there is even an international lifestyle magazine. At contests Julia Morley was regarded as a 'mother hen' figure, resolutely protecting the girls in her charge from the eagle eye of the press, making sure they were being chaperoned while her husband was either, famously, announcing 'the results in reverse order', or organising matters backstage. Mrs Morley allegedly once described herself as a 'self-professed tough bitch'. And yet, despite having been second in command in charge of a competition long accused of being a sexist 'cattle market', she has always supported women behind the scenes.

The phrase 'beauty with purpose' is hers and she banned the revelation of the contestants' vital statistics. But when a reported love affair once hit the front pages of the popular tabloids, she countered: 'I figured that a woman, like a man, is entitled to have a private life and to be respected.


'Good for you, Julia. I agree.

*Halifax Gala Queen 1967*

*National Carnival Queen 1967*

*Blackpool 1968*

*Janet Milner at Morecambe 1969*

*Miss Blackpool 1969*

*Janet Milner at Hallam, Sheffield*

*Miss Sunny Rhyl, 1970*

*Maried Andrew Gordon Stacey, 16th September 1970.*
*Divorced 19th February 1992.*

*Goal Girl Finalist - representing Sheffield United AFC 1971*

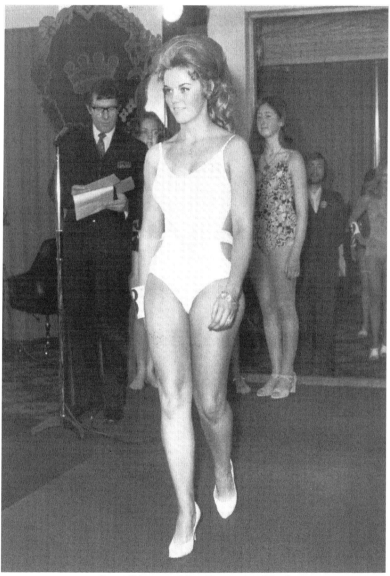

*Janet Stacey at Miss Vegetarian Final*

# CHAPTER 10
# FAME IS THE SPUR

In the Sixties and Seventies contests were mainly fun but the world has moved on and now, in the 21st Century, ambitions have changed, along with attitudes and perspectives.

But before the new millennium began, Diana Hayden, Miss World 1997, succinctly pronounced, allegedly, after being asked by a journalist for her views on today's modern approach to beauty contests: 'You don't bullshit them (the media) and tell them you want to save the world and heal the ozone layer and, you know, be Mother Teresa.'

Obviously, Diane did not believe in mincing her words, later revealing when speaking of the demonstrations in India the year before. 'They threatened to burn themselves and nothing came of it because they were just threats,' she said.

And when informed that a man did indeed burn himself to death, she replied, 'Did he really? What a silly man! All they (the authorities) had to do was ask the girls, 'Do you want to be here or not?'

'You get treated like royalty; you travel first class; live in presidential suites; have bodyguards and chaperones; the prize money is $100,000. Hello! Who's complaining?'

But Diana, a former Femina Miss India, is one of those girls who thinks the Miss World contest has changed, and that the best policy today is honesty. However, the situation was very different in 1964 when Ann Sidney captured the Miss World title. For her, this particular contest was a passport out of her Poole, Dorset home – and away from her parents' expectations.

As I understand it, Ann, who, allegedly, after winning the title, worked as an actress, dancer and singer in the United States, saw the prestigious competition as an opportunity of improving her financial status whilst escaping the conventions of Sixties living.

I read in a newspaper that she thought today's girls had more choices to better themselves by winning the major accolade that came her way, which for her was 'a phenomenal experience and a big, big chance.'

Soon after being crowned Miss World, Ann flew to the United States to meet up with iconic comedian Bob Hope and the pair jetted off to Vietnam to entertain the American troops.

They say travel broadens the mind; it certainly expanded Ann's horizons perhaps better than the further education she craved might have done. But although Miss World became her own particular 'further education', she is reported to have said she would not have done it if she had been a 19-year-old today. 'We've changed; women have changed; everything's changed. And change is good.'

In 1965, another English girl, Lesley Langley from Weymouth, took the crown.

But her pride and joy these days is her daughter Chloe, a former university student, who is currently pursuing a career after taking a year out to travel the world.

The article I read about Lesley revealed that, like Ann Sidney, she considered there were fewer opportunities in the Sixties compared with nowadays, noting that good looks were perhaps relied on more.

'Now there are supermodels,' she is reported to have said, adding: 'There have always been glamorous women cashing in on their looks, so I suppose if you've got it you've got to use it a bit in this world today. And people do; everybody does.'

Both Ann and Lesley were before my time on the catwalk but I had obviously heard of them and had aspired to what they had achieved. However, in their day as well as mine, I have to agree that the options for the various Miss Worlds were not as numerous as they are today. Many girls, though, found it difficult to cope with their newly-acquired fame and once their year of office was over, many of them would return to their homes with a feeling of anti-climax.

Fame had been the spur; they had tasted it but learning to cope with the aftermath could be a bitter-sweet experience for some, depending on their attitude.

However, I must conclude this chapter on a lighter note by relating a true story involving Ann Sidney.

Once whilst appearing with a repertory company in Manchester, she had to take the stage with her teeth 'blacked out' and artificial warts stuck on her face in order to play the part of the third witch in Macbeth.

Imagine her surprise during one of the performances when she heard a youngster in the audience ask in a pig's whisper, 'Which witch is Miss World?'

# CHAPTER 11
# FRIENDLY RIVALS

One of the pleasures of competing on the beauty circuit was meeting the legion of girls in search of fame.

Many of them, like me, came from backgrounds similar to mine. Their careers were similar too, and ranged from hair stylists to students, secretaries to schoolteachers, and even poodle-clippers to petrol pump attendants!

For the most part, however, in the Sixties and Seventies, the majority of girls seemed to hail from the north of England, although London and the south were also well represented as I recall.

But did we all get on with each other? This a question often asked by the media and the general public alike and it would be wrong for me to suggest that everything in the dressing room was sweetness and light.

One girl would 'accidentally on purpose' spill false tan onto favourite costumes of her fellow contestants.

She would wear instant tan and tights, both of which were against the rules. She left the scene in the late Sixties to work abroad as a film extra before returning to England in the 70's with, allegedly, a somewhat inflated opinion of her personal beauty: she genuinely thought she could win any contest she entered.

A favourite ploy of hers was to rush to the front of the stage when the numbers were being given out in order to try and claim the number one ticket. But if she was unsuccessful, she would wait until the end and claim the final one. Our 'friend' was indeed successful in several competition heats but was surprised when she suddenly started losing.

Most of us, however, did not bother what number we had received; even number 13 was regarded as lucky by some, including myself as I preferred it and won many a heat with it.

For the record, I got along fine with most of my contemporaries and we really enjoyed the friendship and competition. To be fair, the odd cutting remark did occasionally rent the air, but they were only minor blemishes amongst otherwise pleasing personnel. On reflection, such behaviour was perhaps no bad thing as it served to prevent inflated egos.

Naturally the girls wore different swimsuits when competing but some had favourite ones; mine was a plain white one with halter neck straps, which I had altered to a shoulder style.

In an effort to 'cash in' when a night by the TV would perhaps have been more appropriate some young ladies would take a risk and enter contests whilst pregnant, sometimes with amazing results such as coming third, but never first.

Reminiscing on my catwalk days, I always retain the feeling there were more happy times than sad. I made lots of friends along the way and travelled extensively, and all of that counted for a great deal as far as I was concerned. I have to say I was lucky in my short beauty career but I did appreciate the experience.

I came to terms with winning and loosing with the resolve I may be lucky next time.

Of course, entrants from Scotland, Northern Ireland and Wales were much in evidence in the Miss Great Britain and Miss United Kingdom events but as a rule, most of my contemporaries were English.

We all shared the joys and heartaches of winning and losing, but happily for us, the successes, more often than not, outweighed the disappointments. And we had fun.

On reflection, the fun was the major benefit as it was important to retain a sense of humour, especially on 'bad hair' days!

Several of the girls who strode along the catwalks at resorts and theatres up and down the land certainly possessed the ability to lighten up many a dark day, the effervescent Wendy Ann George being prominent amongst them.

Wendy, who was crowned Miss Great Britain in 1969, hailed from Littleover, Derbyshire, where her father was a former landlord of the White Swan public house there.

She loved a joke, always had something to say on almost any subject and was the life and soul of the party. Full of enthusiasm, she could be relied upon to tell a good tale, but not dish the dirt.

"Hey, Janet, do you know that so-and-so is going out with so-and-so?" she would inform me.

Usually, I didn't, but all the girls in the vicinity of Wendy would soon be grateful for the information!

Wendy, who now resides in Orrell, Wigan, where she ran a hotel with her ex-husband until a few years ago, proved a success and hit the heights when she was crowned Miss Great Britain in 1969.

Ever resourceful and not the type to be fazed by minor problems, she once, whilst attending a photo-shoot, made a beeline for a pub where she changed from a dress into a swimsuit under the bar, with the landlord serving drinks – and looking on!

And on another occasion, whilst attending a promotional event at a shop, she had to change from her suit into a day dress – but had to rapidly change back into her suit when a fall of soot engulfed her.

Two years ago, Wendy was a former secretary of the now discontinued Royal Lancashire Agricultural Show, working alongside one-time treasurer and contemporary beauty colleague, Valerie Carroll.

A former Miss Sunny Rhyl, Valerie, from Eccleston, Lancashire, was one of those girls whose legs DID go on for ever – and impressed the judges enough to add the Miss Fleetwood 1968 and Miss Preston 1973 sashes to her collection. Today, she lives in Chorley with her property developer husband

Henry and their four children.

Another contemporary and former Butlin's Holiday Princess, was Nanette Slack, a blonde bombshell, who scooped an impressive array of over 200 awards including Miss Anglia TV, Miss New Brighton and Ocean Princess. She was always very competitive and had a passion for winning - and being different; a natural leader, who, if not finishing first, would rather be last, and during a competition, if the other girls were holding their heads straight, she would bend hers. But her tactics must have impressed the judging panels throughout her career, not least in 1968 when she took the Miss United Kingdom title. Now residing in Norwich, she uses her still-good looks to model part-time.

In the Sixties, a girl who was nearing the end of her career as I was beginning mine it became well known for one very obvious reason – her hair.

Jennifer Warren Gurley, a canine beautician from Altrincham, Cheshire, was famous on the circuit for her exceptionally long brown tresses. Her hair - least two-and-a-half feet in length - cascaded like a waterfall down her back to a point just below her waist. Moreover, for a girl 5'7" tall, you can imagine what a magnificent sight that must have looked. It served her well, though, as she was voted Miss England in 1965 and was acclaimed Miss Great Britain two years later.

Whilst Wendy and Jennifer were northern girls making good, a Londoner, June Cooper, who was someone I had heard of a few years before I began on the beauty circuit, had successfully established herself on the nation's catwalks having lifted the Miss England crown in 1958 at the tender age of 16; old enough to win a national title but, unfortunately, considered too young to compete in the Miss UK competition.

My good friend and role model, Diane Parker, enjoyed herself on the circuit and the two of us certainly relished our many journeys around the country, usually with her in the driving seat, competing in the various competitions. She was voted Southport English Rose in 1964, won the Cleethorpes Gala Queen final in 1969 and was crowned Miss Sunny Rhyl the same year, whilst I was fortunate enough to be handed the two latter titles in 1970. Diane spends her time these days concentrating on her hobbies of keeping fit and studying art and antiques. She was my inspiration throughout my relatively short career and I have much to thank her for.

Amongst the other girls I shared many a catwalk with, the stunning Kathleen Winstanley, who won the Miss Lancashire Evening Post title at the tender age of 16 before capturing the Miss Universe title in 1967. She was acclaimed Miss United Kingdom the following year and voted Miss Great Britain in 1970. Originally from Wigan, she now resides in Blackpool whilst her two daughters live abroad in Ibiza and Auckland, New Zealand.

Kathleen, who would often describe beauty contests as 'fun', was also a friend of Hollywood icon Arnold Schwarzenegger, a former Mr Universe, who was no stranger himself to the catwalks of the day; he triumphed in 1968, 1969 and

1970.

Co-incidentally, Jeannie Galston was also one of the 'Terminator's' friends and I shall always remember her raven hair. It was no surprise that she became a Miss She before being crowned Miss British Isles in 1978. Her striking looks later led to her becoming a television model starring in a number of commercials before her successful career in the beauty business ended. But she still remains bitten by the beauty bug today, working as she does in photographic modelling.

She certainly believed life was for enjoying, and set her stall out early to prove that, buying a sports car when she was just 17 years old.

Barbara Ponsford, a fashion model from Dronfield, Derbyshire won a number of titles on the circuit during the late Sixties and early Seventies, including Butlin's Holiday Princess, Miss Variety Club of Great Britain and Miss Sunny Rhyl.

Meanwhile, away from the catwalk, her main interests included the breeding and showing of horses, and riding in point-to-point meetings.

Today, Barbara, who is married to the managing director of a furniture business, tends to spend her free time playing golf and bridge, and attending meetings of her local Sheffield church.

As a footnote to Barbara's successes, it is probably worth recalling an incident involving one of Britain's greatest showmen, Sir Billy Butlin. After being crowned Butlin's Holiday Princess at Brighton in 1970, Barbara's mother

Dallas Hatfield took the Glamorous Grandmother title the following year. Bearing in mind the very reasonable cash prizes involved, Dallas's win prompted a rather down-to earth response from the 'King of Hi-De-Hi' who exclaimed, 'Are there any more at home like you?

I hope not because both of you are costing me a bloody fortune!'

I will always remember too, the tall and willowy Valerie Carroll - mentioned earlier - as a beautiful Lancastrian with loads of charm. She won several titles but, like me, never a national award. However, she possessed a certain air of refinement which she used to good effect throughout her career. Val also had a kind nature and was always quick to help in times of need as I know from first-hand experience. I was competing in a heat of Miss Blackpool in 1970 when I was the victim of a backstage incident. It has to be said that a few of the girls on the circuit were not averse to causing the odd 'accident' or two in a bid to aggravate the opposition! On one occasion, a particular young lady spilt a bottle of false tan – well, needs must when the devil drives – all over my favourite white swimsuit. It was ruined for the competition and the 'apology' I received from my fellow contestant was of little use to me, of course. But Val came quickly to the rescue. "Will this do, Janet ?" she exclaimed, tossing me a pink costume from her bag. "Thanks Val, it will do very nicely. It's beautiful," I responded gratefully. I was, therefore, able to join the rest of my friends around the pleasure beach pool after all.

Another of my close friends in those days was Pam Wood from Rotherham.

She and I shared many a trip to a multitude of venues but her record in competitions was rather unusual, to say the least.

She never won a heat in any competition except Miss Sunny Rhyl in 1970 where she eventually was placed third in the final on what proved to be one of my better days! I was fortunate enough to take the crown that evening and I savoured the moment as there weren't too many like that.

Happily though, Pam scooped the Miss Gala Cavalcade title in Sheffield that summer, ahead of capturing the Miss Cleethorpes title in 1971.

But Pam had one special claim to fame when she was voted the first Miss Yorkshire Television in 1974. This competition is now no more but it did run for a number of years and provided great entertainment for the viewers – and for its unforgettable compere, Richard Whiteley.

A farmer's wife today, Pam opted for the country life after her retirement and now resides in the rolling acres of North Yorkshire.

Bizzarly, my friend Lisa Robertshaw came third in the final of the National Alliance Kleenex Queen contest in 1970 – whilst three months' pregnant! But my best memories of her, centred on the laughs we had. We would literally fall about at some of the things we would say and do, and so bursting into giggle-fits became the norm. Lisa was quite unashamedly a 'wind-up' merchant; she would make 'off-hand' personal remarks to certain of the girls just to test their reactions – and, oh, did some of them react! Having said her piece, she would disappear around a corner to collapse into laughter. The girls eventually got used to her, realising it was just her sense of humour.

On a personal note, however, I was delighted with a beauty tip she once gave me. "Wind your hair around your hand, Janet." From that moment on, I did – and it paid dividends in later competitions.

Another girl I knew well from my modelling days with a Leeds and Bradford agency was Maureen Lidgard-Brown, a petrol pump attendant from the nearby village of Lightcliffe, near Halifax. She was quite a celebrity in my home town, especially following her photographic appearances in the tabloid press during the early Sixties. Her presence at the pumps caused many male motorists' hearts to miss a beat when they filled up at her station. Hardly surprising really, when you consider that she wore a white overall suit and occasionally a low-cut T-shirt! Naturally, she was responsible too, for a huge increase in petrol sales in east Calderdale!

But Maureen had, arguably, one of the shortest marriages ever; it survived just one month before her husband left her and went to live in Spain. However, she is now happily married to an architect and resides in the Cumbrian town of Ambleside where she enjoys fell-walking and playing tennis when she is not wintering in Tenerife.

Maureen, whose sister Jacqui was also a beauty queen, worked at the same garage as Diane Parker, although they were not there together.

Halifax has been fortunate in producing a bevy of beauties over the years, not least the Spink twins, Gay and Zoe, who each found fame on the circuit amassing between them a huge number of titles.

Gay was Miss Great Britain in 1973 and Miss Holiday Princess in 1976 whilst Zoe, who collected more than 50 sashes, took the Miss United Kingdom crown in 1973, becoming Miss Silver Jubilee four years later. Although the girls came into the business three years after I had retired, I mention them because of the Halifax connection; my Mum, Diane Parker's mother and Betty Spink were members of the local Womens' Institute choir. Jam and Jerusalem to the fore!

The twins still live in the Halifax area where mother-of-three Gay is a model, who is married to husband Paul, whilst Zoe, not surprisingly, also works as a model when she is not at home with company director husband Akin and their two children.

Many of the girls on the circuit were tall and statuesque.

Of these, Joy Adams was a prime example, travelling the beauty circuit twice in her long career, which began when she was 16 and ended – for the first time - when she reached 30. But following a two-year break, she took to the catwalk again before finally hanging up her sashes at the tender age of 42!

Indeed, when her age was queried, she would always quote the ruling, saying, "I'm over 21". In her first competitive year, Joy was crowned Butlin's Holiday Princess. Four years later, the Miss Pontin's and Miss Max Factor titles followed. Owner Fred Pontin duly noted her successes, saying, "This has to stop. All we need is for you to win the Glamorous Grandmother competition and we'll have a riot." And he wasn't kidding!

But I can always remember the advice she gave me once, when she told me to start counting backwards after I reached 21!

A contemporary of mine, Carolyn Moore, was a brunette who always wore her hair up or tied back. She would never been seen with her hair down – but it worked for her as she could point to a multitude of successes, including the Miss Great Britain title in 1971.

Yet another Lancastrian, Yvonne Ormes, scooped a basketful of titles between 1967 and 1971, which included Miss Great Britain, Miss England and Miss United Kingdom. As a Miss England winner, she qualified as an automatic entrant for the Miss World competition in 1970, an event which received both publicity and notoriety.

The contest was held at the Royal Albert Hall in London and was famously hosted by Bob Hope, one of the judges being the celebrated film star and actress Joan Collins.

At the conclusion of the event, all the girls lined up on stage only to be pelted with flour bombs by members of the Women's Liberation Movement who had allegedly taken exception to a bevy of beauties enjoying themselves! "A cattle market that degrades women" was the cry of the aggrieved objectors, who also hurled stink bombs and ink bombs, some of which hit their targets but not before Miss Grenada, Jennifer Hosten, had been declared the winner on that unforgettable night in London.

In the mayhem, Mr Hope managed to take evasive action but Miss Collins was less fortunate, a football rattle hitting her on the head but, happily, causing little damage.

Yvonne, who is now a hairdresser in Nantwich, later revealed that the experience was a frightening one and there was bitterness that the night had been ruined by the 'libbers'.

I must say that, certainly in those days, we entered competitions for fun, which in itself was totally harmless – and we felt that there was more than a hint of jealousy on the part of a section of the female population who somehow took umbrage against us parading in swimsuits.

Cheshire air-hostess Judith Wannop never won a national title but her good looks brought her close on a number of occasions, most notably between 1966 and 1969 when she was placed third, fourth and second respectively in the Miss England, Miss Southport English Rose and Miss Blackpool competitions.

One contestant who took beauty pageants, and just about everything else, very seriously was Oldham girl Carol Richmond. Studious to a fault, she was a beautiful brunette who won the Queen of the Nidd title in 1969 before landing the Sheffield City Council-sponsored Miss Gala Cavalcade the following year. But she must have needed something of a sense of humour before being crowned 'Queen'; she was, after all, paraded around the streets of Knaresborough held aloft on beds carried by students on each corner – of the beds that is!

A keen supporter of Oldham Athletic Football Club, she leads a more carefree life at home in the Lancashire town with her solicitor husband.

Another Cheshire girl, Kathleen Winstanley, was also a circuit regular and eventually had her day in the sun when, in 1970, she was voted Miss Great Britain. Today, she has her own catering business.

Liverpudlian Ann Halton, Miss Prestatyn 1968, was a runner up to myself on many occasions, including second place on the podium in the Miss Sunny Rhyl final. In her competition days she was a student but these days she is employed as an art teacher and portrait painter in Southport, Merseyside.

Ex-dental nurse Gillian Taylor, hailed from Wilmslow, Cheshire, but these days she resides in Bristol she was a dental nurse and is now a housewife, with three children and three grandchildren. She gained the Miss Cheshire Rose title in 1961, was Miss Bristol a year later, and scooped a big one in 1963 when she became Miss Great Britain .

One contestant, Kathy Anders, was a successful heat winner, although fame seemed to be passing her by. But in 1974, she hit the heights when she was awarded the Miss England crown following the disqualification of Helen Morgan from Barry, Glamorgan. Unfortunately, Helen was a married mother - and that was against the rules of the competition.

But, by being placed second to the Welsh girl, Kathy was promoted – and duly became Miss England six months after the holding of the contest.

Popular with the public, she had an engaging temperament and would always see the best in people. We were all stunned when we learnt she had been fatally injured in a car accident on her way back home from celebrating the news of her win.

Finally, I recall the vivacious Margaret Triggs-Butler, a former Miss Southport and Miss Liverpool, claiming an impressive 23 minor titles throughout her career. Always ready to assist with sound advice, Margaret was an asset to the beauty business, helped along by a cheery humour and many a well-placed joke.

Happy days indeed – and in the company of girls I am pleased to call friends.

# CHAPTER 12
# EXPLODING THE MYTH

As I mentioned in the previous chapter, I was fortunate enough to enjoy the company of many girls on the circuit during my days on the catwalk. However, I am aware that many people cannot avoid wondering whether, as a group, we all 'gelled' together. I would be very naïve to state that a certain amount of arrogance, back-biting and jealousy did not occasionally rear their ugly heads from time to time but personally, I encountered very little.

In truth, some girls – but only very few – would delight in delivering the odd cutting remark in an attempt to undermine the confidence of their targeted victims, usually students; entrants in town for the day who had been encouraged to enter by their boyfriends or parents, or agency girls. It was perhaps, allegedly, a case of trying to eliminate the competition to allow only the circuit regulars to win. I suppose it is fair to say that some girls did not really enjoy seeing the occasional newcomer upstaging them and walking away with the top prize. However, there were instances of the so-called 'fleeting' girls taking a liking to the life of the beauty queens and joining them 'on the road'. Needless to say, they were soon accepted as they too, had become regulars.

For my part, I was lucky that my good friend Diane Parker took me under her wing when I started and treated me as a circuit girl - and not an outsider - straight away. But we all recognised beauty and respected those who were fortunate enough to possess it. So in all conscience, it would have been churlish and unfair to deny any pretty girl the chance of her day in the sun – and a bit of fun for good measure.

# CHAPTER 13
# MORE ACCOLADES

In April 1969 a London agency offered me modelling work at the Leeds College of Art. At first this was day dress, and swimsuit, but they also asked me to do 'life' which, Diane informed me, meant nude. I refused, and was immediately struck of their list of girls. I then knew what sort of agency it was. And it wasn't for me!

Thank goodness for the beauty business. The season had begun well enough in June with a second prize in a Miss Blackpool heat of Miss United Kingdom.

And in the same month, I qualified for the final in the first heat of the Miss Sunny Rhyl contest and went home with £10, half a dozen Britvic glasses and an Irish linen tablecloth! As you can tell from this, the organisers really knew how to spoil us in those days!

As in the previous year, I again entered the Miss Britain heat at Tiffany's in Sheffield and was fortunate enough to get top spot in the first heat in my area and took home a prize of £10, a Hoover hair dryer, a £3 Max Factor make-up kit, a 12-month course at Sheffield studio Gateway to Health – and automatic entry to the September finals of Miss Britain in London.

In the Sixties the prizes on offer varied greatly between competitions. But it was important to get a sash. Success bred success as is the case today, of course. Therefore no prize – although some were mind-numbingly cheap – could be ignored.

More Miss United Kingdom heats followed with chequered results before I finally qualified with the magic 'first' at Burnley for a place in the September final.

The heats for Southport's English Rose also started in June and I was lucky enough to be selected for the final in the sixth heat together with Margaret Triggs-Butler. Cash prizes were awarded along with hairdressing and make-up vouchers from Andre Bernard to be used at the final in September. As Miss Burnley, I was interviewed on Radio Two and asked the question, "How did it feel to be one of the two remaining girls left behind the curtain?" I replied; "It doesn't bother me. There will always be another year, and therefore another chance to win."

Once again, a philosophical approach had to be employed to hide the obvious disappointment at not being selected. It really was, and still is, a case of 'c'est la vie'.

Undaunted, Diane and I were soon hitting the road again and found ourselves at the Queen of Queen's contest in Oldham, where I claimed third spot in the heat; Diane was fourth on the night.

I began to wonder how I would fit all these finals in. Luckily, all of them, so far, happened to fall on different evenings.

In September, Dennis Lever along with my parents and I, again attended the final of Southport's English Rose but I was not lucky enough to be selected amongst the winners.

However, in the audience I recognised a young 10-year-old girl who approached me and asked if she could have her photograph taken with me. She informed me: "This summer I have followed you and been at of the contests you have appeared in. I'd like to take part in a beauty parade myself and even become a model like you!"

Comments such as these boost any flagging morale – and make the effort expended for possible success all the more worthwhile.

The cameo with my new friend also, hopefully, illustrates that opinions are just that. A different panel of judges might have made alternative choices on the night – and that is what we all had to believe.

So, I wished my charming admirer all the very best in her quest to hit the heights in the beauty business. She seemed very pleased with life after our little chat and smiled sincerely before rejoining her parents.

The following month, one of Dennis's fellow photographers offered Diane and I some modelling work. However, as one learns in the beauty business, some things are not always what they seem and after one session Diane warned me off because they were asking me to drop a shoulder strap – which could be construed as bordering on topless – and therefore possibly, porn.

Not surprisingly, the two of us refused any further work.

There was still other work to be done, though, so, undaunted, I carried on with the busy schedule and the next day entered the Queen of Queens contest in Oldham with Diane.

The following day I travelled to Morecambe for a heat of Miss Great Britain and picked up second prize. But when was the marvellous first going to be mine?

Later, whilst enjoying dinner in a local restaurant, Davilda Corry called our attention to a poster for the Miss Nightclub of Great Britain contest to be held at the Windmill in Ainsdale, Southport.

Davilda, Barbara Garvey and myself decided to take part in the contest, afterwards staying overnight at Barbara's home. In the event, Davilda and I became joint winners receiving a monetary prize and a bottle of Dubonnet each.

In August, Andrew escorted me to the final of the contest and I won twelve months' free membership at the Warren Golf Club, Penistone, a bottle of Dubonnet, a box of Contrast Chocolates, together with a cash award to complete my 'prize'.

In October, I modelled at the Motor Show as well as again merchandising for Players. I was also employed as a toy demonstrator at Redgates for the pre-Christmas period.

For me and all the other girls competing on the circuit in the Sixties and

Seventies there was always plenty of work. We knew we had to make the most of our looks whilst we could. But if we had them, we could 'open doors' for ourselves – and supplement our sometimes tight resources by becoming legitimately engaged in promotional work.

The year finished, though, with a win in a heat of the Alliance Village Queen at Pembroke Hall, Worsley this allowed me to go forward to the regional final to be held at the Grand Hotel, Manchester in November where I was eventually chosen as one of the eight finalists.

# CHAPTER 14
# MY BEST YEAR

Amongst all my years on the beauty scene 1970 proved to be my best. And it began well with modelling work at the Boat Show in Leeds in April.

I attended the Jersey Holiday Queen competition at Sheffield Tiffany's but could only manage third spot in the heat. And I was placed third again in the Goal Girl competition at Burnley Football Club, Turf Moor held in a March event.

Later in the month I won the Sheffield heat of Miss England at the Silver Blades Ice Rink and therefore I qualified for the final. My reward was £10 and a Triumph swimming costume to wear as a finalist. At the final I reached the last seven.

They say that "haughty pride cometh before a fall" but in this business it was, certainly in those days, sometimes a case of swallowing a mountain of pride. I remember this maxim in particular when recalling events such as Mr Smith's Easter Bunnies contest at a night-club in a Manchester back street. For the record, on that occasion I was placed third but it was more a case of doing the business and leaving as quickly as possible to avoid any possible unsavoury behaviour from the customers.

In April, my Bradford modelling agency asked me if I would like to be one of the girls involved in helping John Gilks, a local struggling archaeologist, to get some well-earned publicity. After he had discovered a medieval village site near Huddersfield, an article appeared in the Daily Sketch and was later reported on ITV's Calendar programme, and the Halifax Courier ran a story with a picture taken in my garden by Dennis Lever.

Come the merry month of May I took part in Sheffield's Gala Cavalcade where I was placed third behind Barbara Ponsford and winner Carol Richmond.

The Miss England final was held in September and on this occasion I reached the last seven, dressed in my new red crimplene dress with a keyhole of gold sequins. Yvonne Ormes was crowned the winner but afterwards, David Jacobs interviewed me on BBC Radio One to find out how I felt not being a winner. I answered briefly, but optimistically: "It's disappointing but, I might win next year."

Meanwhile, a new contest, Miss Ambre Solaire, found its way on to the beauty list in 1970 and I was fortunate enough to be awarded the winner's sash at the Sheffield heat in May. The prizes were attractive too; a week in Portugal awaited the final winner - and spending money as well.

Whereas I was not wholly enthusiastic about entering this fledgling contest, it was Diane who prompted me to try for it, as there was the princely sum of £25 to be won in the heat.

"I think you should go for this one, Janet. It's £25, if you manage to win the heat," said Diane. I did, but I could not attend the final owing to the work commitments of my then fiancé Andrew.

On a Wednesday afternoon in June, Pamela Wood and I decided to drive to Rhyl instead of trying our luck in Morecambe or New Brighton. The move proved beneficial for me, at least, as I won a heat of Miss Sunny Rhyl with a cash prize of £10 plus a hair appointment and shoes for the final in September.

I felt rather sorry for Pam who, that day was not placed at all but she said it was just the luck of the draw. This was the philosophy all of us had to adopt on the circuit: win some, lose some; but battle on.

One day the following month, however, Diane and I drove to Skegness, picking up Pam Wood and Barbara Ponsford en route for the Miss Skegness contest.

It turned out to be fruitless journey in the event. Somewhat deflated after each of us had 'drawn a blank' we decided to stay overnight before travelling to Cleethorpes for the town's Gala Queen contest, a full one-day event, where Diane reached the final six with Pamela being placed third, Barbara second and myself first. We all received cash prizes and bottles of spirit too! My prize was a bottle of champagne, which I opened at dinner, and each of the girls toasted the health of the others.

But there is a little tale to tell regarding the champagne. For my sins I gained something of a reputation on the circuit for making the odd gaffe – nothing major, or course, but big enough for others to take notice! After being awarded the winners sash, the mayor of Cleethorpes then presented me with the bottle. I was so overjoyed at scooping the main prize that I unwittingly remarked: "Oh, I've never seen one as big as that before in my life!"

You could have touched the embarrassment with a short stick but everyone saw the funny side fortunately, and all was well in the end - I hope. I am a Sagittarian after all, so the odd tactless remark is allowed!

In fact, I suppose I could say the good people of Cleethorpes did forgive me as the town's local newspaper, the Telegraph, published a photograph of Andrew and myself taken at our wedding reception held at Holdsworth House, Ripponden near our home town of Halifax the following month.

And the link with the resort continued, when, in December of that year, we were invited to join the judging panel for the next Cleethorpes Gala final to be held in July 1971.

Perhaps the most important thing, though, was that the long trail my friends and I had taken, had, at last, proved profitable.

But the feeling of success never endured, and resting on one's laurels was not an option. We all had to take to the road again and hope for the best.

It was around this time that Andrew suggested I retire from all competitions whilst I was 'at the top' as he put it. I agreed but, as I had qualified for various finals, I needed to attend them. We decided jointly that I should fulfil my obligations for the coming year following which I would call it a day.

Meanwhile, buoyed by my latest triumph in the Lincolnshire resort, I decided to 'go west' to Morecambe once again where, during the last week in August, I was selected for the final of Miss Great Britain. Could success at last be around the corner? Alas, it was not to be as I only eventually reached the final 16. Kathleen Winstanley won by the toss of cricket great Freddie Trueman's coin as the judging panel was split and Freddie provided the solution to a very sticky problem.

I have to say that I am not a great believer in Fate but I decided to employ a little help in the form of my lucky silver slipper charm, which, I had received from Andrew for my twenty-first birthday. It clearly did the trick, though, as I won the last heat of Miss United Kingdom at Blackpool, the event being judged by my favourite comedian of the time, Billy Dainty, whose marking paper I have kept to this day.

As luck would have it, later that September, Pamela Wood and I made it to the final of Miss Sunny Rhyl, where the judges, found in my favour for the winners sash. Carolyn Moore took the runners-up spot whilst my Rotherham friend claimed the third prize.

Whenever I think of the Miss Sunny Rhyl contest I tend to reflect that I always seemed to do better inside buildings rather than outside parading around swimming pools. Indeed, because of the inclement weather on the day, the final was held in the local town hall.

I must also add that I could say the same about judging panels, too, as panellists of, shall we say, more mature years would appear to favour me rather than members of a younger panel.

Later in the same month, Pamela, Dawn Cooke and I attended Southport's English Rose final where I reached the last 12 with Dawn securing the title. Of the other contestants that day Kathy Anders became Miss Britain 1971.

In March of that year I decided to change my eating habits - and became a vegetarian. Coincidentally, somewhere in Sheffield I picked up an entry form for the Miss Vegetarian competition, filled it in, sent it off - and forgot all about it. I later received a letter informing me that the one-day event was to be held at the Bonnington Hotel in London.

It proved to be a successful journey for me to the nation's capital as, although I failed to win, I at least captured the runners-up spot and selected a simulated fur coat to the value £45 from Beauty Without Cruelty as part of my prize. But the change of diet was only temporary, as I decided it did not suit me! Also included in the prize was a society dinner dance at York with all expenses paid. The coat was then worn every winter even when I became pregnant with the buttons being altered to allow for the bulge!

# CHAPTER 15
# MARRIAGE AND DIVORCE

At the fair age of 23, on Thursday 16th September 1970 at three o'clock in the afternoon, I married Andrew Gordon Stacey at St. Jude's Church, Halifax.

My dress was white-corded satin, I carried a white maribou muff with pink roses and on my head I wore a ring of maribou fur.

The Reverend M J Walker conducted the ceremony at which my cousins Jennifer, Diane and Christine were bridesmaids whilst an old dancing school friend Angela Hughes was my chief bridesmaid.

Andrew's brother David was his best man; his friends Peter and Duncan the groomsmen, and old family acquaintances Ian and Howard Johnson took the roles of ushers.

After the ceremony the reception was held at Holdsworth House in the town, after which Andrew and I left for our honeymoon in Benidorm, and on our return moved into a Redcar Road flat in the Sheffield suburb of Crookesmoor. It has to be said that life could have been easier as, at the time, I was the main wage-earner whilst Andrew continued to study for his degree at technical college, having only his student grant as income.

But in between beauty contests, I worked as a model primarily for a local agency, in addition to demonstrating, selling and merchandised cigarettes, mushrooms, toys, gardening products and cosmetics. In the beauty business in those days, contestants needed to be flexible.

Travelling was often irksome but all my contemporaries were a dedicated bunch, although, following my marriage, it was Andrew who would drive me to contests all over the country, rather than my girlfriends.

On many occasions, we would arrive at a resort early in the day, prior to me taking part in an event in the afternoon. Later, we would either travel to another competition, or find a place to stay the night before dashing off to yet another contest the following day. Abundant stamina, therefore, was a definite requirement for a beauty queen in the Sixties and Seventies.

Andrew, in those days, had only to attend two lectures a week at Sheffield Polytechnic where he was taking a PhD in metallurgy, and so had the opportunity to escort me to competitions on days when he was not studying. Despite my change of status – I now became Janet Stacey instead of Janet Milner – people who followed the progress of beauty contestants still recognised me, which was gratifying, at least.

Soon after, I became a beauty consultant at Boots the Chemist in High Street, Sheffield, working for Elizabeth Arden Cosmetics after being spotted using a specialised technique introduced by ICI (mixing compost – I kid you not) with television personality and the BBC gardening expert Percy Thrower.

At home, the first few years of my marriage went smoothly before I learned a hard lesson that a wife has to play many parts; cooking and cleaning, managing the home, supporting her husband in his career pursuits, and being an unpaid diplomat, personal assistant and saleswoman of a product I knew nothing about - wire.

I had also to go out to work and all this was expected as my duty. Unfortunately, it began to take a toll on my health but I tried to show willing - until 1972 when I became pregnant.

Being true to my promise to Andrew, I gave up work and competitions eight months into labour to look after my first daughter, Helen Odette, who was born in Doncaster on 7th April 1973.

Thankfully, though, my happy event did little damage to my figure, a situation which proved beneficial six months later when a friend suggested that I enter the local heat for the Gazette Queen of Clubs contest which was held at Campsall & District Working Men's Social Club. In the event, Susan Smith of Bentley and I jointly won our heat which led to appearances in the final.

Obviously, Andrew had no idea I had taken part in the competition but I informed him on my return home. My earlier 'promise' had been forgotten as he congratulated me and wished me well for the ensuing final.

However, I could not attend the 'big event' as I fell pregnant again with my second daughter Sarah Ruth. I was in hospital for six months with depression after Sarah's birth, my other daughter Helen staying with my mother whilst

Andrew's mother looked after Sarah until I came home.

Sadly, though, my marriage began to deteriorate after giving birth to Helen but before the arrival of Sarah. Andrew and I were certainly happy for the first two years of our union, but many factors conspired over the following 19 to send our relationship into a tailspin before we finally divorced in 1992.

Because of pressures encountered in the marriage, Andrew decided I would embark on 12 electroconvulsive treatment sessions, which resulted in a temporary cancellation of all my competition memories. Had it not been for my mother keeping my scrapbook cuttings, I would not now be able to remember anything. But happily, since the end of the treatment all my memories have now returned.

I really wanted to return to work but as my children were fairly young, I undertook voluntary employment at the local hospital, collected for church charities, and finally joined the Neighbourhood Watch Scheme to fill my time. In the end, though, I reverted to type becoming a beauty consultant with Avon Cosmetics working from home.

# CHAPTER 16
# MY PENULTIMATE YEAR

I could never have imagined that the following year would turn out to have something of a football feel about it – but it did. For after winning a photographic heat of Goal Girl 1971, I appeared in a photo-shoot at Bramall Lane, the home of Sheffield United, wearing the number two shirt of their popular right-back of the period, Len Badger. I have to say I was delighted to wear his jersey but declined to wear his shorts as well!

In the event, I opted for my own patriotic 'hot pants' in red, white and blue, which hopefully, did not clash too much with the red and white stripes worn by the Blades' players.

I had entered the national contest, which was sponsored by a weekly soccer magazine to find Britain's 'Top Dolly of the Terraces'. (Can you believe these titles?!)

I had only been married for eight months but had been a fan of the team since moving to the Steel City after our honeymoon. In the event, I failed to win the final but at least I had the enjoyment of wearing Len's shirt!

Meanwhile, Andrew had secured his Higher National Certificate in metallurgy and was making quite a name for himself in the Sheffield Sunday

Imperial League playing for Polystaff, the Polytechnic staff team (naturally!), and for Ecclesfield Church in the South Yorkshire Amateur League.

For the record, he appeared in one game in which there were three penalties awarded within five minutes. After saving one attempt at goal for his side, he was adjudged to have been off his line for the kick. But he held his nerve to save the retake – and help his team to a 4-3 win.

Sadly though, my interest in the round ball game has dwindled since those heady days at Bramall Lane but I still take an interest in the Blades' results whenever and wherever I happen to see them.

Back down to Earth again, my Bradford agency sent me to the Spar supermarket in Elland, a town near Halifax which had achieved fame during the Sixties as the home of the Gannex raincoat, a favourite choice of apparel for the then prime minister, Harold Wilson.

The promotion of a new product, the aperitif Shloer, was the reason for my visit there and on my arrival, I was introduced to the manager, Wynn Standeven, who just happened to be my Dad's wartime friend. "Hello!" he said, in a surprised manner. "I didn't know it would be you they were sending." I was equally surprised and replied, "It's great to see you too – and I'll try to sell as many bottles as I can."

I worked at the supermarket for six weeks during the spring, selling the grand total of 350 cases – with a dozen bottles in each case. On one occasion, a local luminary from a mansion in the fashionable Halifax suburb of Skircoat

Green arrived at the emporium in a chauffeur- driven car.

She tried one of the sample glasses of Shloer on offer to customers and appeared well pleased with the product. "This is capital. I know it will be appreciated by my ladies at afternoon lunch and at evening dinner," she enthused - and with that, she promptly ordered 100 cases!

At the end of my tenure, my Dad's old friend said, "My word, haven't you done well?" I responded, "I hoped you would be pleased," happy that I had put a smile on his face.

Indeed, we reminisced often at our respective homes, especially at Christmas-time – and the lady from Skircoat Green would always be mentioned.

Returning to the circuit, I entered Miss Beauty Cavalcade at Sheffield's Owlerton Stadium in the summer. The June contest was an annual one-day event held on a Saturday and in 1971, the worthy winner from the 16 entrants was my good friend Pam Wood, who received £50 for her efforts, with Leeds girl Maureen Gibbons third, whilst I split them with second spot.

I took a minor placing in each of several contests throughout the summer months before entering the  Miss Sea Legs competition in 1971.

I duly made my way to Sheffield's Top Rank Suite one Saturday evening in September to try my luck in this brand-new contest along with other hopefuls. None of us knew what to expect but the competition, held in connection with the 'Sheffield Goes To Sea' exhibition at the Cutler's Hall, offered excellent prizes.

Following the judging, I was fortunate enough to land the winner's sash together with the first prize of a cruise holiday to Africa which, much to my disappointment, I couldn't take owing to Andrew starting his new appointment at British Ropes in Doncaster.

I felt it important to support my husband but my Mum held a different view. On learning of my success, she exclaimed, "Why don't you take me?" I replied that the two of us would try to recover the cost for ourselves.

"Well, if you think you can do it, you do it," she said haughtily. My Mum could do 'haughty' when she felt like it!

Although we did make an effort, because we were dealing with a foreign company, we finished up with no recompense whatsoever. Such is life, I suppose.

However, there was better news for the runner-up, Pamela Richards from Barnsley; she was promoted to my spot and duly tripped off to the Dark Continent herself.

Following a promotional engagement working with the well-known BBC gardening personality, Percy Thrower, I had some good news from two of the buyers employed by Boots the Chemist.

One told me I had registered impressive sales figures whilst working on my Leeds agency's books for ICI. "In view of this, said Miss Hodgson, "I may have some good news for you,"

She told me she had a vacancy with Elizabeth Arden. "Training will be given as well. Do you think you could handle it?" "Yes, if you are training me, I can handle it," I replied with a mixture of pride and fear.

"Can you start in a fortnight?" she added.

However, the 14 days in London were really a training period. So what she was asking me was if I could begin work right away. I replied that I could, and was promptly despatched to the nation's capital where I was holed up in a staff flat in Regent Square for the duration.

On leaving London as a fully qualified beauty consultant, I was immediately employed at the company's High Street outlet in Sheffield city centre. Miss Hodgson, who worked at the branch, was firm but fair. A 'taskmaster' of the old school, she would say, "The last person to have this job returned excellent figures – and I expect you to do at least the same." No pressure there, then! I stayed at the branch for 20 months, eight of which I was pregnant with Helen, my first daughter, but I thoroughly enjoyed the experience – including the redoubtable Miss Hodgson!

I recall one occasion when I arrived at work one morning only to be greeted by Miss Hodgson with the words, "Have you come to work dressed?"

Feeling somewhat dispirited, I blurted, "How could I? My uniform doesn't fit me because I'm pregnant, and I do live in Doncaster."

Miss Hodgson concluded the short discussion. "See that you come to work tidy, in future." she said before walking away. Fortunately, one of my colleagues was good enough to take me upstairs to the staff room and 'tidy' me up before going downstairs to the shop where I stayed all day. Redoubtable indeed!

Earlier, in March, I decided to enter the photographic heats of the Miss Vegetarian competition. Dennis Lever had taken pictures of me in Morecambe at a shoot on the beach there the previous year and these were sent along with an application form to London. One of the requirements for the contest was that all the entrants had to be vegetarians. I can honestly say that I had avoided meat for at least a year before the competition was held.

I then completely forgot about the contest until I received a letter from the Vegetarian Society of the United Kingdom informing me I had been chosen in a shortlist of nine finalists to attend the Bonnington Hotel, London in September 1971. I had won second prize - £10 and a simulated fur coat worth £45.

A 19-year-old London fashion model, Jane Thomas, won the final and was crowned by Rupert Davies of Inspector Maigret fame, Rosemary Sinclair, of Welwyn Garden City, taking third place.

The three of us on the podium each received a simulated fur coat in nylon fabric from Beauty Without Cruelty. I also won a £10 cheque, and an invitation to a dinner dance at the society's expense in York the following May, which I duly attended and certainly enjoyed.

## CHAPTER 17
## THE CURTAIN FALLS

A barren year from the point of view of beauty contests was my lot for 1972 as I was too busy working at Boots.

Out of necessity I took a complete break from the circuit to concentrate on my pregnancy. In fact, I continued to work until a month before giving birth to Helen in April 1973.

Balancing work and pregnancy was somewhat hectic for me, to say the least, in those days. Taking regular daily train journeys between Doncaster and Sheffield was fraught with problems in itself; I remember falling off the train at the former Midland Station in Sheffield twice whilst still carrying Helen. A very kind porter – unbelievably, the same one on each occasion – rushed to pick me up with the words 'Whoops! Be careful there. Mind how you go.'

During the stocktaking period, I would use the travelling time once a month to fill in order forms and before I could pause for breath, as it were, I had reached my destination and had to rush to alight from the train; hence my tumbles.

All these experiences were new to me, of course, and such was their effect on my figure and my life that the only competition I was to enter before finally bidding a fond farewell to the catwalk was a heat of the Gazette Queen of Clubs in September the following year.

The local heat of this heady contest was held one Tuesday evening at the Campsall & District Working Men's Club at which nine contestants took part. Luckily, I became one of the two girls chosen – the other being Susan Smith - to progress to the quarter-final stage of the competition, having made a Herculean effort to reduce dress sizes from 18 to 12 for the contest  after giving birth to Helen.

Unfortunately, before the quarter-finals came along, I fell pregnant again - with Sarah – and, as a result, could only wonder as to what might have been the outcome if I could have continued. To be honest, I was more that a little disgruntled when I found out from my local GP that I was expecting my second daughter;

The spirit of competition still burned brightly, but I had been thwarted on what was to be the last hurrah.

On informing Andrew that I would be unable to attend the final, he replied, 'What's more important, this contest or your baby?' adding, 'I think your baby's more important.' In truth, he was right and I had to agree – and let commonsense prevail.

So it was then that my swansong took place at a local venue; it was as though I had literally travelled full circle in a career spanning an all–too-brief six years.

Although I was happy being pregnant again, I remember feeling that a void had opened up in my life. I reflected that I would miss all the girls, who had shared the highs and lows of the beauty business – and I said as much to my good friend Diane Parker.

An activity such as parading in front of the public in bathing costumes and fine gowns – in all manner of places and in all weathers! - made me feel important and special; winning a heat or, better still, a final, certainly put the icing on the cake, making the effort well worthwhile.

I know my colleagues felt the same way and it was something of a wrench to leave a wonderful set of memories. But life changes and I had to change with it.

# CHAPTER 18
# LIFE AFTER DIVORCE

At first, I was desperate and thought there was no life after divorce but then discovered otherwise.

Initially I went dancing alone but later a girlfriend or my eldest daughter, Helen, would accompany me. But I would only dance with friends until my confidence returned.

One crisp winter's evening, around Christmas of 1987. I was carol singing for charity when Andrew informed me that my father had been taken into hospital suffering from a heart attack. A month later after we had talked about his military escapades during the Second World War he passed away.

The funeral service was at the local church and the congregation sung one of my father's favourite hymns 'Jerusalem'.

And within two years, Andrew's own father had similarly died of a heart attack on the very day his son remarried, his mother passing away eighteen months later.

Our financial deliberations since my divorce in May 1992, took five years to resolve but happily all matters regarding it are now settled.

I continued to study throughout my divorce and happily gained a useful selection of qualifications in business studies.

My evenings during study were spent at local working men's clubs, with my friend. One place springs to mind – Thurnscoe. It was there where the secretary used to do a spot and would introduce himself with the words, 'Just excuse me a minute while I play with my organ!'

Sadly, my mother died on 21st May 1999 and I miss her so much as she was such a friend. She fell and had to have a hip operation. While she was in the infirmary she caught an infection and died of peritonitis. She was always there offering comfort and guidance when I needed it – and sometimes when I didn't - but I shall always remember her with affection.

With a friend from college, I joined a singles club and made many new friends, and we now enjoy the theatre, cinema, playing bowls, badminton, Sunday walks, dinner-dance evenings and holidaying together.

In September 2000, a gentleman called John  joined my singles club: we became friends with the same interests – walking, gardening, history, and musical theatre. At New Year, our friendship blossomed into a relationship and we now talk of eventually moving in together when he sorts his family out. He is divorced and has a 23 year-old son who is a pub manager. He also has two daughters one aged 20, training to become a nursery assistant, and an elder married daughter of 39 with two children who is a carer for her disabled husband.

So therefore, it would appear life is good for me at last; it has been somewhat traumatic over a number of years but I have happily brought some order into it, and for that I am very grateful.

# CHAPTER 19
# TODAY'S BEAUTIES

In 2006, Edith Barton-Harvey, a Sheffield University sociology student, took part in the Miss England contest.

There was nothing exceptional in that event but the first few years of the 21st century have witnessed a sea-change in a competition which has altered, almost beyond recognition from those carefree days of the Sixties and Seventies, enough to make a significant difference in the attitude of the competitors.

It is said that comparisons are odious but, to be fair, in my opinion, the girls today seem to be more vivacious and perhaps more beautiful than they were in my era.

The feminist attitudes of the Seventies and Eighties - when protesters regularly disturbed the peace at beauty contests in an effort to promote their mantra that the contestants were parading in "meat markets" - have given way to a new breed of feminism in which the participants themselves are adopting a hard-line stance in a bid to use every attribute in their armoury to achieve their career aims.

Indeed, Miss Barton-Harvey sees beauty competitions as a way of positively enhancing her career, believing that she should take advantage of what she has to show on a catwalk.

Many of her contemporaries feel the same way; Big Brother, the X Factor, Miss England – what's the difference if it gets them noticed, they would argue. My own view on this matter is that I feel if today's beauties wish to use their bodies as well as their brains to help them in their careers – and life in general – then good luck to them. But I have my reservations.

Feminism in the early 21st century has changed considerably since the Sixties with girls now expecting to create all manner of opportunities for themselves, including parading on catwalks, in a bid to be recognised. In short, the publicity will help or at least, that's the plan.

For my part, I consider the beauty business has today become more of a cattle market than it was in my day. For example, it is alleged that heat winners for the Miss England 2005 pageant had to learn how to pole-dance before competing in the final. I feel this to be a retrograde step, and degrading for the girls involved.

In the Fifties and Sixties, the Miss World contest reached a television audience of over 14 million people whereas today's competition, although televised, does not reach anywhere near that number. So from that standpoint, perhaps viewing attitudes have changed to the extent that maybe the greater choice of channels has something to do with it.

Because of the television coverage, it could be argued that beauty competitions today are less popular than they used to be.

Organisers of the many tournaments have changed too. In particular, Angie Beasley, a former Miss Brighton, took over the reins of the Miss England competition from Julia Morley in 2006, the year in which Eleanor Glynn, from Oxford, won the coveted title.

For the record, in the previous year, the contest was won for the first time by a Muslim entrant, Hammasa Kohistani, a student from Uxbridge, Middlesex, while in 2007, a North Yorkshire beauty therapist, Georgia Faye Horsley of Malton, took the crown.

As I mentioned earlier, the beauty business has taken on – it would probably argue – a more sophisticated look in that, in addition to the beauty and brains couplet, it now offers contests within contests. For example, Miss Earth International, for which there is a crown, is now subdivided to include a further three sections, namely, Miss Wind, Miss Fire and Miss Water! Such a contrivance was not around in my day. And to add to the 'confusion,' there is now a Miss India UK, and, would you believe, even a Miss Maxim UK, which chooses pornographic 'stars'!

It is only my personal opinion, but such a competition as the last named should be banned; it is disgusting and degrading to women.

Personality and good looks played the major parts in a girl winning a heat or a final in the heyday of competition – although even a rather plain-looking girl could progress in a contest if the judges thought she was bubbly, whereas today, it appears the organisers have added the extra dimensions of brains and talent, thereby increasing the pressure. There was really no stress for my contemporaries or myself: we just enjoyed ourselves doing something that we liked. So, on balance, I suppose it was easier taking part years ago. It was arguably more fun, though.

# CHAPTER 20
# MEMORIES

On reflection the six happy years spent in the beauty business helped me grow into a mature, young lady, broadening my outlook on life and giving me a better sense of perspective.

But my memories of those catwalk days will always be with me and, indeed, help to keep me going if ever I feel in sombre mood.

I especially remember a tall, blonde-haired contestant who wore tights under her swimsuit – until instant tan was invented. She would often spill the tan 'accidentally on purpose' over favourite costumes of other contestants.

But one day she had to stop using the tan because we had all complained to the competition hostess. That same afternoon the weather came to our aid and finally stopped her little tricks, as when she was halfway round the pool, it began to rain, washing the tan away and giving her skin a blotchy appearance. Our 'friend' only realised her misfortune when she stood in front of the judges. But by this time it was much too late; she had no chance! We all broke out into fits of laughter; the biter had been bitten. Oh happy days!

*Janet, Helen and Sarah Stacey 1977*

*Janet Stacey and John Smith 2010*